Picture Perfect

Mowing Techniques for
Lawns, Landscapes, and Sports

David R. Mellor

Ann Arbor Press

Ann Arbor Press
310 North Main Street
P.O. Box 20
Chelsea, MI 48118
www.sleepingbearpress.com
Ann Arbor Press is an imprint of Sleeping Bear Press

Printed and bound in the United States.
10 9 8 7 6 5 4 3 2 1

Library of Congress Cataloging-in-Publication Data
Mellor, David (David R.)
Picture perfect : mowing techniques for lawns, landscapes, and sports / by David
Mellor
 p. cm.
Includes biographical references (p.)
ISBN 1-57504-151-0
1. Turf Management. 2. Turfgrasses. I. Title.

SB433 .M39 2001
635.9'642–dc21

2001022648

This book is dedicated to:

Denise, my lovely wife and best friend, whose tireless energy amazes me, and to Cacky and Tori, our daughters, who are my inspirations. I love you three more each day. I am fortunate and proud to have each of you in my life!

"Talking Turf" with my daughters during batting practice. I always enjoy when the girls help me on the field. Photo courtesy of Ron Vessley, MLB © 1996.

In memory of my brother Terry, who loved his yard and taught me to reach for my dreams.

Like most people, my life has had challenges and detours. I learned from my mother, brothers, wife, and family that facing challenges head on and overcoming adversity strengthens you.

My dad died when I was three years old. A loving mom and two older brothers, who had the added responsibility of filling in as dad, raised me. Their time and attention served me well. I have wonderful memories of growing up that I wouldn't trade for anything.

The passion for baseball is a family affair. My grandfather, Bill Mellor, played Major League Baseball in 1902, for Baltimore. One family treasure is the letter inviting him to play in a 1939 "Old Timers" game at Fenway Park benefiting the Veterans of Foreign Wars. Other participants included Ty Cobb, Babe Ruth, Cy Young, Tris Speaker, Walter Johnson, Honus Wagner, George Sisler, Grover C. Alexander, Eddie Collins and Larry "Nap" Lajoie (grandpa's close friend). Unfortunately his poor health prevented him from attending. Growing up, I loved baseball. My goal was to follow in my grandpa's footsteps to Major League ball, and I had earned opportunities to play in college already. My dreams were detoured shortly after I graduated from high school when I was hit by a car. I was crushed. Then, an accident in physical therapy dashed all hope of ever playing again. During the next three years I had seven surgeries on my right knee.

Thanks to my mom, my brothers Terry and Chip, and my wife, whom I met in October 1982, I didn't give up. They helped me through difficult times by keeping me focused on the positive and encouraging me to reach for my dream of working in Major League Baseball. Since I couldn't play baseball anymore I pondered other options.

My brothers advised me to find a career I loved where I would look forward to going to work every day. Growing up I had cared for my neighbors' lawns, loved being outside, and loved baseball, and my favorite subject in school was science. I put these thoughts together. Someone had to take care of the baseball fields at Major League Stadiums. Why couldn't it be me?

In the fall of 1984 I contacted George Toma of the Kansas City Royals. He's one of the "Godfathers" of sportsturf. He was kind enough to share his time and knowledge with me on how to get my foot in the door of sportsturf management. He stressed education combined with experience. I was already studying landscape horticulture at The Ohio State University, so I added agronomy classes to gain soil and turf knowledge. But I also needed hands-on experience.

My brother Terry, who was living in Milwaukee, said that I if could get an internship with the Brewers I could live with him to save money. Gary VandenBerg and the late Harry Gill gave me a chance in April 1985 by hiring me as an intern. In 1987 I interned with the Brewers, the San Francisco Giants, and the California Angels. After graduating from Ohio State in December 1987 I went to work full time for the Milwaukee Brewers. In January 2001, I was hired by the Boston Red Sox to become Director of Grounds at famous Fenway Park. My job is the next best thing to playing baseball. Being behind the scenes at the ballpark is exhilarating. I still get butterflies in my stomach when I walk on the field today. Thanks to everyone at the Brewers and the Red Sox, I can honestly say I found the job my brothers urged me to find, because I truly do enjoy going to work each day.

In October 1995 I was involved in a freak accident at the ball-park. A confused woman trying to drive onto the baseball field hit me with her car. She told the law enforcement officials she thought she was doing a movie stunt. Because of this accident and the earlier one I have had 18 surgeries on my right knee. At 32 years old I had a total knee joint replacement. I've learned to deal with difficult situations and pain through these trials and tribulations.

Nothing, however, can compare to the loss of my brother and best friend, Terry, who died in July 1998. He, his wonderful wife Pat, and my family had spent a great Sunday together. At the end of the day we said our "normal" goodbyes. Two days later Terry died of a massive heart attack at the age of 42. There are many things I wish I had said to him and shared with him. Since that tragic day I have learned to appreciate each day and say "thank you" and "I love you" to those close to me. I have learned to take time to recognize what's important, to keep my priorities in order. Take the time to tell those in your life how important they are to you. Life can change in a split second. Enjoy each day to the fullest and find time to have fun with those you love.

With these thoughts in mind this book is also dedicated to all the people who have touched my life over the last 37 years. I thank you for the experiences we shared together.

ACKNOWLEDGMENTS

I gratefully thank my friends, colleagues, and mentors, who have bestowed their knowledge on me throughout my life. The experiences we shared helped me with this book.

Special thanks go to my wife, Denise. Your dedicated assistance with this book's development played a vital role in its completion. I really appreciate your incredible friendship and love. You are the best and you always make me smile.

To my daughters, Cacky and Tori, your understanding while Mom and I worked on the book was wonderful. Thank you for your patience, good humor, and suggestions during the writing of the manuscript. You two are totally awesome. You give me the gift of joy and you will always be in my heart.

Thank you, Mom. As life goes on I continue to realize how you sacrificed so that Chip, Terry, and I wouldn't have to. Since Dad died you had dual roles as mom and dad. Your strength and unconditional love never wavered. I have wonderful childhood memories and I reflect on your mentoring every day. I will try to pass on to my children the values you instilled in me.

To my brother Chip, I have looked up to you (not literally, since I am taller!) all my life. Thank you for filling my life with humor and love. Your input on this book is greatly appreciated—especially the part about my graduate teaching assistantship while at OSU, even though that part didn't make it into print.

To my brother Terry, Here's a thank-you I wish I had said when you were alive. You taught me so much about life and about professionalism. I thought of you often while writing this book and continue to benefit from your wisdom daily. Thank you also, for being such a positive influence in my daughters' lives. I miss you more than words can express and I treasure the memories we created together. As you know, we made it to Fenway!

To Aunt Kaka, your love and support have been invaluable to me. You are like a second mother. For this I thank you.

To Gary VandenBerg, you were not only my boss, but a true friend. You gave me opportunities to experiment and learn how to best present beautiful patterns. Thank you for your guidance, support, and the unending opportunities you share with me. Thanks for your comments and suggestions on the manuscript.

To Mr. Allan H. (Bud) Selig, Wendy Selig-Prieb, and Laurel Prieb, A special thank-you for your understanding during the learning process with the many patterns we tried over the past eight seasons at Milwaukee County Stadium. I appreciate the feedback and support from each of you.

To Alata Pullins Kallas, thank you for your editorial assistance with the manuscript. Your advice and counsel significantly improved the final manuscript. Your love and friendship mean so much to Denise, Cacky, Tori, and me.

Thank you to Joe Mooney, John Buckley, Joe McDermott, and the Boston Red Sox for the incredible opportunity to be Director of Grounds at the famous Fenway Park.

Thanks to Tim VanWagoner, Mary Lou Hall, and Barry Patton, important members of my focus group, who reviewed the manuscript. Your suggestions helped me communicate my thoughts better.

Thanks to Ground Crew members Kirt Bakos and Joe Vopal for all your help with patterns throughout the years. Your pride and attention to detail on the field and in our patterns shows through in the photos in this book.

I also want to thank all the Milwaukee Brewer and Boston Red Sox Ground Crew members with whom I have had the pleasure to work. You have all played a valuable role in enabling us to execute striking patterns.

To Melinda Myers, thank you for your words of encouragement, which helped get me started on this book. While I thought it was admirable, I thought you were crazy when you told me you wrote your book from 2 A.M. to 8 A.M. Little did I know that I would start writing at 2 A.M. every day for four months. But you were right: It cut down on interruptions and, more important, by writing in the wee hours of the morning I didn't have to take time away from my family.

Thanks to my friends in the media who helped with research and contacts, and to the Cooperative Extension Agency, whose publications served as a backbone for several chapters of this book.

Thank you to Skip DeWall, Lynne Johnson, Felicia Macheske, and the staff of Ann Arbor Press/Sleeping Bear Press. Skip, you were always there for me when I called. You made writing this book a pleasurable experience.

Thanks to Dr. Joe DiPaola, who planted the seed with Skip for this book after hearing a speech I presented at the Ohio Turfgrass Foundation in December 1998.

Thanks to Troy Smith, Jack Carr, Nolan Meggers, Jim Puhalla, and Eugene Mayer for your assistance, and to the many friends and colleagues who graciously donated photos of their patterns for this book. These spectacular images are fantastic! Unfortunately, I couldn't include all the photos that were sent to me. When I started this project I didn't realize how many talented people also love making patterns and how much pride they take in their work.

Picture Perfect

Mowing Techniques for
Lawns, Landscapes, and Sports

CONTENTS

Chapter 1

INTRODUCTION

The wave of excitement sweeping the turf care industry is all about mowing patterns. This isn't just another passing fad. The growing popularity of striping patterns among athletic field managers, home-owners, and landscape contractors is exploding at an incredible rate. I have noticed a whirlwind of interest in patterning over the past seven years. Striping designs have become a signature of excellence, and they have helped set a higher standard of expectations for the aesthetics of turf.

Patterns have even garnered the attention of the art community. Photographic slides I took of patterns produced at Milwaukee County Stadium during the 1997 and 1998 baseball seasons were included in an internationally touring art exhibit: "The American Home Lawn: Surfaces of Everyday Life," organized by Phyllis Lambert, Director of the Canadian Centre for Architecture and the architectural firm of Diller and Scofidio from New York City. The images were projected onto a wall, with each pattern dissolving into the next, resulting in a magnificent kaleidoscope of scenic green murals.

Patterns have become so popular that video game manufacturers are programming patterned grass playing surfaces into their sports games to add realism. Just a few years ago computer programmers and consumers were satisfied with just a plain green background.

Widespread national media coverage reflects the depth and intensity of the interest in patterns. Articles about my work with mowing patterns have appeared in many publications, including *Smithsonian Magazine, The Wall Street Journal, USA Today, Popular Mechanics, Grounds Maintenance, International Baseball Rundown*, the front page of the *New York Times* "Art and Leisure" section, the *Toronto Globe, Lotus International, Wisconsin Trails, Sports Turf, Athletic Turf Maintenance and Technology, Landscape Management*, and the *Milwaukee Journal Sentinel*. In May of 1999 I was featured on "CBS News Saturday Morning" as "Milwaukee's

Diamond Cutter." This story presented points on "Creating 'Cutting Edge' Fields of Dreams." The story also ran on their web site, cbs.com, combined with "Mellor's Mowing Tips."

People often ask me, "What makes the grass look so pretty at ball parks and golf courses? How can I make those awesome patterns on my lawn?" The answers are not as mysterious as you might think. This book answers those questions and many more. Included are tips from the pros on ways you can make your grass the envy of all. You can create a picture perfect turf by following the steps I outline in this book. After reading *Picture Perfect: Mowing Techniques for Lawns, Landscapes, and Sports* you will be capable of making a fashion statement through your lawn.

Lawn striping and patterns created by mowers have been around for years. The first mower, developed in England in the 1830s, made stripes on the grass when it cut. It was a reel-type mower with a large roller behind the cutting blades. The roller was used instead of wheels to transport the mower. As a result, the roller would bend the grass blades in the direction it was traveling, producing a striped pattern. In Victorian times people loved the look of stripes on their lawns. Mower advertisements of the time featured the banded finish and striping these mowers made. With developments in technology mowers have come a long way. Through the years they have come in all shapes and sizes. Recently lawn and garden manufacturers, realizing the sincere interest in patterning, have focused on developing mowers that not only provide a clean, safe cut, but also create pretty patterns as they mow.

Simplicity is the one manufacturer of homeowner mowers who has included rollers as part of their Free Floating™ mower deck for more than 30 years and markets the equipment's ability to make patterns. Striping kits as attachments for professional rotary mowers are also being offered by other companies. As with the homeowner mowers, the kit includes a roller attached behind the cutting units, just like the first mower and professional quality reel mowers, which provide striping by bending the grass blades in the direction the mower travels.

People worldwide have seen eye-catching patterns on television while watching baseball, golf, and other sporting events. When watching game highlights on "ESPN Sports Center" or "CNN Headline News," you can't help but notice the incredible turf patterns in the background. These patterns easily catch your attention. They show the pride and the tender loving care of the turf manager. The attention patterns receive has prompted some to paint patterns on their Astroturf® fields. Turf patterns have generated interest and enthusiasm among homeowners excited about making designs themselves on their property. I'll outline steps in this book that will build the basic skills you'll need to become a pattern master. With this knowledge and some practice you will be surprised how much fun you'll have and how easy it is to make a spectacular striped turf. I'll share my experience and show you step by step how to get started. Then I'll describe more complex patterns, but these will also be easy to follow. In a short time you'll be able to reproduce designs in the book and even dream up special designs that will showcase your site in the best way. You'll develop your own style and your own favorite designs. The more you practice, the more proficient you'll become. Only your own desire and imagination will limit the designs you can make.

Whether you choose simple traditional designs or elaborate patterns, making your own patterns is a great way to express your pride, and it will surely add value to "curb appeal." You aren't restricted to doing just a few patterns, either. In fact, it's important for the overall health of your turf to rotate mowing directions approximately every two weeks. This will prevent a "grain" in the grass—when grass starts to grow at an angle. Changing your mowing direction will also help prevent wear from the mower tires and the cutting units, which will occur if you do not rotate designs.

Patterns help make memorable first impressions. When fans take their seats at a stadium, one of the first things they notice is the grass. Likewise, when your friends and family drop by, the first thing they notice is your lawn. You have only one opportunity to make a first impression. Seize that moment. Give your friends and family the bonus of a dazzling pattern. A customized pattern on your grass adds a touch of class to your home.

Patterns can be used to aid turfgrass health, increase aesthetic value, and imply line boundaries on sports fields. Patterns can also be used as a motivational tool for employees, allowing them to learn the best ways to conquer the challenges each turf may offer. Welcome employees' suggestions. Before long the employees will catch the pattern fever and start a friendly competition among themselves.

The smell of freshly cut grass is so appealing that it has even been used in cologne. The aroma brings back great memories for me. The smell of freshly cut bermudagrass takes me back to my Uncle Bob's putting green just outside his patio doors in South Carolina. For years I thought the aroma was that of my uncle's ever-present cigar. Now I know it was his freshly cut bermudagrass. Like many kids, I mowed lawns to earn money. My older brother Terry taught me at an early age to mow in a straight line because it affected how well the yard looked when completed. Even though I mowed with a rotary mower, which didn't have a roller to make a true stripe, I learned to make sure the wheel marks were straight. That pride in attention to detail is something I have carried on throughout my life.

I studied at The Ohio State University, earning a Bachelor of Science in Agriculture in December 1987, specializing in Agronomy/Turfgrass Management and Landscape Horticulture. While in college I worked at Scioto Country Club golf course. I realized quickly that when I did my best mowing, the higher profile greens and fairways would find their way onto my assignment list. I used reel mowers with rollers and saw the dramatic stripes they made. While in college I interned for the Milwaukee Brewers, the San Francisco Giants, and the California Angels major league baseball clubs. Upon graduating in 1987, I started full-time with the Milwaukee Brewers. Through the years I have honed my skills through practice. I have always admired well-manicured turf and the special patterns that are chosen for athletic fields, golf courses, and

Set-up for Paul McCartney concert at Milwaukee County Stadium in June 1993. Photo by David R. Mellor.

home lawns. The professional look that is attained with patterns is obvious. Patterns can dress up even a tired-looking piece of turf.

Of course, you will need to follow proper turfgrass management practices so that you will have the ideal surface on which to develop your works of art. I have included a section on the basics of turfgrass care so you can also have lush turf to enhance your patterns. In this book you'll see my pictures, along with those of some talented friends who were kind enough to share images of their favorite designs. There is an unspoken, friendly rivalry among pattern masters that brings out the best in each of us. Once you start making patterns you can join this fraternity, delighting in perfecting your next masterpiece.

In 1993, after Paul McCartney played a concert in Milwaukee County Stadium, I learned the amazing response a special mowing pattern can produce. It rained throughout the setup, the concert, and the takedown of the big show. The huge stage was set up in the outfield, covering about one-quarter of the grass. The field was carefully protected by over 2,000 sheets of plywood used to create double-layer access roads for the forklifts employed to haul the steel used in the construction of the stage. The remaining parts of the field were then covered with a special felt-like blanket (GEO® textile) and Enka® mat to protect the turf from the thousands of chairs and dancing feet. Despite our efforts to protect the turf, the stresses of the concert and the inclement weather caused visible damage. After the concert, we

Outfield turf damage from the Paul McCartney concert in Milwaukee. Photo by David R. Mellor.

first worked to ensure that the field would be safe and playable. Once that was accomplished we turned our attention to the aesthetics of the outfield grass, where turf in front of the stage—which had been under the plywood road—showed the most wear. We mowed a pattern on the outfield to camouflage the damage, but were still not pleased. We also used other techniques mentioned later in this book to try to hide the damage. They all helped, but we still weren't satisfied.

With support from my talented boss, Gary VandenBerg, I created a complex pattern on the infield grass to draw fans' attention away from the outfield damage. The positive response that night was overwhelming. The New York Yankees were in town and their announcers did not mention the damage from the concert—but they complimented the mowing pattern on the infield grass often. During the following weeks we received phone calls from viewers across the United States and Canada who had seen the pattern on television. Fans and colleagues alike asked how the design had been created on the turfgrass. They wanted to know if they could create such patterns on their own lawns. I realized then that a pretty mowing pattern not only adds beauty but can be used as a tool to hide damage or draw someone's attention away from a location that can't be brought up to par.

This unique infield design was used to draw the eye away from the damaged outfield turf.

Photo courtesy of Tom Nielson

Thanks to new developments by mower manufacturers and the secrets I share in this book, homeowners, athletic field managers, landscape contractors, and golf course supervisors can now create unforgettable mowing patterns. Whether you've never done a pattern or do them often, there is information in this book that you can use, to add pizzazz to your turf. If you've ever wanted to mow like they do in the majors, this book is for you. You'll have fun learning both basic and complex concepts, and you'll earn the admiration of colleagues, friends, and neighbors with a turf that begs the question: "Wow! How did you make your grass look so great?" It will be up to you whether you lend them your copy of *Picture Perfect* (Better yet, buy them a copy!)

This book is organized by first explaining the basics of turfgrass management. These chapters are separated into the following subjects: Test Your Soil, Turfgrass Establishment, Fertilization, Common Nuisances, and Mowing Recommendations. These easy-to-understand chapters will provide you with a strong foundation in proper lawn care practices. You will be able to use this valuable knowledge to grow a lush, healthy turf that will be the ideal canvas on which to create your lawn art patterns.

The next section—consisting of Making Turns with Your Mower, Equipment—Tools of the Artist, Preventing Traffic and Wear Problems on Your Turf, Techniques to Help Hide Damaged Turf, Useful Tips, How Patterns Are Created, and Pattern Basics—will walk you through everything you need to know to make gorgeous patterns on your grass. These chapters focus on basic procedures and important strategies to learn before starting your designs. In Pattern Instructions, the last chapter in this section, I will teach you ten patterns, ranging from simple to unique. The user friendly instructions include step-by-step procedures and diagrams that explain techniques that will help you master these designs and provide a foundation of skills that will help you create special patterns of your own. Pattern Instructions will also answer all your questions on exactly how patterns are applied to grass.

I've included a section with extraordinary high-quality photographs of patterns created by turfgrass professionals on baseball, soccer, and football fields, golf courses, and home lawns. These incredible photos are excellent examples. You can try one, or choose parts of different patterns and execute your own new version. These photos will inspire your creative energies, and with some practice your turf will be the talk of the town.

The next chapter is Photograping Your Lawn Art. The tips included in this chapter will explain how to take better pictures and how to put together a portfolio of your grass masterpieces.

In the chapter entitled Three Challenging Situations, I relate some unusual happenings that have occurred during my career in turfgrass management.

Finally there is a handy Resource section, which provides phone numbers, addresses, and web sites for college and university turfgrass programs, equipment and fertilizer companies, and turf professionals. Through these resources you can get answers to questions and gather information on equipment, fertilizers, disease and pest management, and numerous other topics to aid you in your overall turf care program.

Chapter 2

TEST YOUR SOIL

A soil test is a simple, inexpensive way to take the guesswork out of lawn care.

Before you plant grass seed or fertilize your lawn, get a free soil test kit from your local Cooperative Extension Office, dig up a soil sample, and have it tested by the Extension Service. The soil report will tell you in plain language whether you need to apply lime to restore the soil's natural chemical balance. It will also tell you what kind of fertilizer is needed and how much you should use. For best results, carefully follow the instructions given for the soil test. Private companies also do soil testing. These can give detailed reports and recommendations, but they may be expensive. Have your soil tested every three to five years.

The purpose of a soil test is to supply you with enough information to make a wise fertilizer and soil amendment choice. A soil test will provide information on pH, available phosphorus, potassium, calcium, and magnesium. Soluble salt tests can be run on request. The results of the soil test will be mailed to you, along with recommendations on what kind of fertilizer or amendments (material added to aid plant growth by improving soil conditions) should be applied for economical growth of the desired crop or specific plant. The best pH levels for healthy grass range from 6.0 to 6.5. A recommendation included with soil test results will indicate how to reach the proper pH level. Submit your sample in the fall, prior to planting or tilling, so that needed lime or other soil amendments can change the pH over the winter.

The accuracy of the test is a reflection of the soil sample taken. Be sure your sample is representative of the area to be treated. Sample the soil from ten random areas to a depth of about 8 inches. Avoid sampling unusual areas, such as those near gravel roads, manure or compost spots, brush piles, or under eaves. Place the samples in a clean plastic pail or container and mix the soil thoroughly, then transfer 1 cup of mixed soil to a container and take it to your local Extension Office. The results will be mailed to you.

Existing nutrient content and soil texture must be determined before efficient recommendations can be made as to the amount and type of fertilizer or other material that should be applied to a lawn. The amount of fertilizer, lime, and other amendments recommended for soil improvement should allow optimum growth without undue risk of polluting the natural runoff. It's important not to apply more than is recommended. If time of year or season of application is a part of the recommendation, these guidelines should also be closely followed. This will ensure the greatest plant response with the least chance of plant damage or drainage water pollution. Fertilizer, lime, and other amendments washed off by heavy rains contribute to stream pollution.

Soils vary greatly in their properties and in their suitability for different uses. Many of the differences in soils relate to the geologic parent materials and the local topography. The main soil types are sand, clay, silt, and loam.

Sandy soil feels very coarse and grainy. Water drains through it very quickly. As a result, sandy soil dries out rapidly.

Clay soil is very thick, like putty. It holds water like a sponge. Clay soil doesn't dry out as fast as sandy soils, but when it does, it becomes hard and very solid, making it quite difficult to break the soil surface with a shovel.

Silty soil is between sandy and clay soil. It holds water well but doesn't dry into a hard, solid mass.

Loam is the ideal mixture of sand, clay, and silt. Through the addition of organic amendments, loam can become the perfect soil for your vegetable garden.

Remember that a soil test is an easy way to determine your turf's nutritional needs. It's simple, low-cost, and provides information about needed amounts of nutrients for healthier turf.

Chapter 3

TURFGRASS ESTABLISHMENT

There are four aspects of turfgrass establishment: selecting a turfgrass that is adapted for that particular area; preparing the soil for planting; planting—which may include seeding, sodding, plugging, or sprigging; and care and maintenance of the newly planted lawn to ensure successful establishment. The Chicago-based, not-for-profit group The Turf Resource Center (TRC) found that several common mistakes made by homeowners in the establishment process—including cultivar selection, fertilization, mowing, and watering—contributed to problems with turfgrass.

Turfgrass Selection

Proper turfgrass selection is one of the most important factors in the successful establishment of any turf area. Not all species and cultivars will perform equally when placed in widely differing geographical areas and climates. The turfgrass you select should be adapted to your area and meet the level of turf quality you desire. When deciding which turfgrass to use, consider the level of traffic and the amount of care you will be able to give your lawn. Some selections will put up with more abuse than others. Some grasses will tolerate—or even demand—low levels of fertilization and still be presentable.

Turfgrasses are divided into two categories: cool-season and warm-season. These categories are based on their climate adaptability. Some areas are in the "transition zone" of grass growing, which can make cultivating beautiful turf a struggle regardless of your choice. This "transition zone" is approximately on a line horizontally across the United States, including the cities of Kansas City, St. Louis, Cincinnati, and Baltimore. The winters are too cold for warm-season grasses and summers are too hot for cool-season grasses. Cool-season grasses grow best there in the spring and fall. Their optimum growth is between 60° and 70°F. Hot weather causes them to go dormant and turn brown until cooler weather and rainfall revive them. On the other hand, warm-season grasses look their best at the height of summer. Some years these grasses do not green up in the spring until mid to late May. The first hint of frost in the fall causes them to turn dormant/brown for the rest of the fall, winter, and early spring. They are established in the early summer.

One way to exploit the best qualities of the different types of cool-season grasses is to sow a mixture of compatible turfgrass species. Look for cultivars that are best suited to your region and site.

Soil Preparation

The key to establishing a successful lawn is proper soil preparation. The soil preparation is the same whether planting seed, sprigs, stolons, or sod.

The Soil Test

The first step in soil and seedbed preparation when establishing a new lawn is taking and submitting a soil sample. Submit a soil sample at least three weeks before the date you want to seed. Soil test kits are available at County Extension Offices. You can find your County Extension Office listings in the blue government pages of the phone book under "County Governments." A basic test includes soil type (percentage of sand, silt, and clay) analysis and recommendations regarding nutrients. Soil testing will determine whether the soil pH and nutrient levels are in a range that favors turfgrass growth. The soil test report will indicate needed amounts of fertilizer or lime.

Clean and Rough Grade

Clear the planting area of coarse debris, such as sticks, rubbish, and stones. Treat the area with a glyphosate herbicide, such as Roundup® or Kleenup®, which will kill all existing vegetation. Read and follow all label directions. Labels for these products advise a seven-day waiting period between application and seeding or sod installation. Sometimes tough, deep-rooted perennial weeds will require retreating, resulting in an additional week of waiting time.

After the treated area has browned out, it's safe and even helpful to mix the dead weeds and grass into the soil as a free source of organic matter. If extensive grading is needed, remove the topsoil and stockpile it for replacement after the rough grade is established.

The subsurface may become compacted during rough grading, especially if the ground is wet. This compacted layer must be broken up before replacing the topsoil. A spring-tooth harrow works well on lightly compacted soils; a small rototiller may be needed for more heavily compacted sites.

Replacing the Topsoil

Once the subsurface is established, replace the topsoil and spread it uniformly over the area. Allow for soil at least 6 to 8 inches in depth after it has settled. This means placing about 8 to 10 inches of topsoil over the subsurface. Improve the soil by adding organic matter, which improves water retention in sandy soils and drainage in clay soils and reduces fertilizer leaching.

Deep Tillage

Rototilling loosens compacted soil and improves the speed and depth of rooting. A tractor-mounted or self-propelled tiller will adequately till the soil, but take care not to destroy the existing trees in the lawn. Cutting too many tree roots during soil tillage can severely damage or even kill a tree. Trees can also be suffocated by deeply covering the roots with soil. If additional soil is necessary at a tree base, construct a "tree well."

Fertilization

Just prior to seeding, level the soil and apply the fertilizer as recommended by the soil test. The County Extension Office can provide additional information on ways you can design and adjust your fertilization program based on the soil test results. Be sure to follow the procedures your testing lab recommends. This will help ensure accurate samples and results. Once your samples are tested, a report will be compiled on your results, with suggestions for improvements. These recommendations can be used as a guide in selecting what fertilizer analysis would be best suited for your plants' needs.

A general recommendation is for a "starter " fertilizer, specially formulated to contain higher amounts of phosphate to aid germination. If a water-soluble, quick-release source of nitrogen is used, do not apply more than 1 pound of actual nitrogen per 1,000 square feet.

If a water-insoluble source of nitrogen is used, such as urea-formaldehyde, you can apply 3 to 5 pounds of actual nitrogen per 1,000 square feet prior to planting.

Once the soil is properly prepared, it's time to plant.

Seeding

The appropriate turfgrass species or blend must be chosen and a high-quality seed lot obtained. The three main factors affecting turfgrass establishment from seed are: planting procedures, mulching, and post-germination care.

Buy Quality Seed

Successful establishment requires purchasing top-quality seed. Law requires that each container of seed list the turfgrass species and cultivar, purity, percent germination, and weed content. Purity indicates the amount (as a percentage) of the desired seed as well as other seed and inert matter. Check the crop and weed seed content on the label. Quality seed will have no more than .05 percent weed seed.

Germination percentage tells the amount of seed expected to germinate under optimum conditions. Try to purchase seed that has a purity of 90 percent or higher and a germination of 85 percent or higher. Don't try to save a few dollars buying cheap, low-quality seed. The little money you save now will cost much more money and time in the future due to poor results. Investing in high-quality seed will be less expensive in the long term since it's less likely to require over-seeding or resodding.

Seeding Methods

Many seeding methods can be used, including planting by hand and using mechanical equipment for large turf areas. Evenness of seed distribution is important for overall uniformity. After the seedbed is well prepared and leveled, rake the entire area with a garden rake. Apply the seed mechanically with either a drop spreader or a rotary spreader. Mechanical seeders provide a more uniform distribution than hand seeding.

For best distribution, sow one-half of the required seed in one direction and then apply the remainder at right angles to the first seeding. When seeding with very small seed, such as centipedegrass or bermudagrass, it's helpful to mix the seed with a carrier, such as corn-meal or an organic fertilizer. This helps distribute the seed evenly.

With a rake, mix the grass seed with the top ¼ inch of soil. Then roll the seedbed with a light or empty water-ballast roller to ensure good seed-to-soil contact.

Mulch the seedbed to prevent soil erosion, retain moisture, and prevent crusting of the soil surface. The most commonly used mulch is straw, but it's important to use weed-free straw. One bale of straw (60 to 80 pounds) will cover about 1,000 square feet. The straw can be removed when the grass reaches a height of 1 to 1½ inches or can be left to decompose if it isn't spread too thickly. Two good seed mulches on the market are Seed Aide and Penn Mulch. These prod-ucts are small pellets made of compressed paper/wood fiber that swells when wet, holding moisture to aid in germination. Follow the label directions for suggested application rates. Peat moss or aged sawdust isn't good mulch for seeded lawns. These materials compete with the seed for water and are slow to decay.

Water the lawn as soon as possible after seeding. Watering with a fine spray will help seed germinate, but be sure to prevent washing or puddling.

Care of a Seeded Lawn

After Seeding
Proper watering is the most critical step in establishing turfgrasses from seed. Apply water frequently so that the soil is moist, but not excessively wet. Supplying water two or three times a day in small quantities for about two to three weeks will ensure adequate moisture for germination. If the surface of the soil is allowed to dry out after the seeds have begun to swell and before roots have developed, many of the seedlings will die. As the seedlings mature and their root system develops, the frequency of watering can decrease, but the volume should increase, so that the entire root zone is moistened, not just the soil surface.

After Germination
During the establishment phase, a number of practices can be employed to help ensure a uniform, dense turf. A combi-

nation of mulching and irrigation is key in successful turf-grass establishment. If a straw or hay mulch is used, be sure to monitor the grass seedlings for shading. If the new seedlings show yellowing, lightly rake away some of the mulch.

Mowing

Begin normal mowing practices when the turfgrass seedlings reach a height one-third higher than the normal mowing height. It's important to maintain a sharp cutting blade to avoid pulling these seedlings out of the soil.

Fertilization

A light application of nitrogen fertilizer, made when the seedlings are between 1 and 2 inches tall, will enhance the establishment rate substantially. Apply approximately ½ pound of actual nitrogen per 1,000 square feet and water it well into the soil. Avoid excessively high-nitrogen fertilization.

Irrigation

The surface of the soil where seeds are germinating and seedling growth occurs should be moist at all times. Water often enough to keep the seedbed moist but not saturated, until the plants can develop sufficient root systems to take advantage of deeper and less frequent watering. Soils that haven't been mulched will dry out quickly. Less irrigation is needed when mulch is used. The quantity of water applied will be small and should be maintained for at least three weeks following planting. As the turfgrass matures, reduce irrigation to a maintenance level to promote a deep root system.

Weed Control

Timing of weed control practices is critically important once seeds have germinated. Herbicides target unwanted plants but may also stress the grass plant, reducing its growth rate. Most herbicides are somewhat toxic to newly germinated turfgrass plants. Delay applying post-emergence herbicides for weed control as long as possible after seeding. Follow recommendations found on pesticide labels closely with regard to timing of application after planting. Diligent care of the young lawn during the first two or three months is crucial for its overall success.

Vegetative Planting

Vegetative planting is simply the transplanting of large or small pieces of grass. Solid sodding covers the entire seedbed with vegetation. Spot sodding, plugging, and sprigging refer to the planting of pieces of sod or individual stems or underground runners called stolons or rhizomes. Most warm-season turfgrasses are established by planting vegetative plant parts. Exceptions to this include centipedegrass, carpetgrass, common bermudagrass, and Japanese lawngrass (*Zoysia japonica*), which can be established from seed.

Sodding

Sodding is more expensive than sprigging or plugging, but it produces an "instant" lawn. It's recommended when quick cover is desired for aesthetic reasons or to prevent soil erosion. Establishment procedures for sod include soil preparation, obtaining high-quality sod, transplanting, and post-planting care. Sod can now be purchased in a variety of sizes. Big roll sod is often used on athletic turfs. It has fewer seams and results in fewer chances for bad hops or stepping in a seam. Due to their size and weight, there is less chance of shifting under an athlete's feet, making them safer.

The primary objective in sod transplanting is to achieve a quick rooting into the underlying soil. Factors that influence quick rooting include proper soil preparation, adequate moisture in the underlying soil, and transplanting techniques that minimize sod drying.

Install cool-season grass sod any time of the year as long as the soil is not frozen. If done in the fall,

An example of big roll sod commonly used on sports fields resulting in fewer seams, better footing, and a safer playing surface. Photo by David R. Mellor.

transplanting should be completed early enough to allow root growth into the underlying soil before cold weather arrives. Winter sodding is done when conditions for root growth are not favorable. The grass may or may not survive the winter, depending on temperatures.

Dampen the soil just prior to laying the sod to avoid placing the turf roots in contact with excessively dry and hot soil. Establish a straight line lengthwise through the lawn area to reduce the need for short pieces when installing sod. The sod can then be laid on either side of the line, with the ends staggered in a checkerboard fashion. A hand sod cutter or sharpened concrete trowel is handy for cutting pieces, forcing the sod tight but not overlapping, and leveling small depressions.

Do not stretch the sod while laying it. The sod will shrink upon drying and cause voids. Care must be taken to prevent gaps between sod rolls. Stagger lateral joints to promote more uniform growth and strength. On steep slopes, lay the sod across the angle of the slope. It may be necessary to peg the sod to the soil with stakes to keep it from sliding. Immediately after the sod has been transplanted, roll or tamp it. This will eliminate air spaces between the soil and the sod. Roll perpendicular to the direction the sod was laid.

Make sure to water newly transplanted sod immediately. Wet the soil to a 3-inch depth to enhance rooting. Do not let the soil dry out until a good union between the sod and soil surface has been achieved. Light, frequent applications of soil topdressing will help smooth out the lawn surface.

Soil Preparation
Soil preparation for sodding is identical to that for seeding.

Sod Quality
Before buying the sod, inspect it carefully for weeds, diseases, and insects. Check with the grower and source to acquire sod grown in a soil type similar to that in your yard or field. Store the sod in a cool, shady location until used, but do not store for more than 1 or 2 days. Purchase a little more than needed so bad spots can be cut off. Try to install it as soon as it is delivered.

Care After Transplanting Sod
In the absence of adequate rainfall, water daily, or as often as

necessary, during the first week and in sufficient quantities to maintain moist soil to a depth of at least 3 inches. The sod should then be watered lightly during midday hours until rooting into the underlying soil has taken place. Deeper, thorough watering can then be done as the roots begin to penetrate the soil.

Do not mow until the turfgrass sod is firmly rooted, and not too wet. The mowing height and frequency on newly sodded areas should be the same as normally practiced on established turfs.

Sprigging

Sprigging is the planting of stolons or rhizomes of warm-season grass varieties in furrows or small holes. A sprig is an individual stem or piece of stem of grass with no adhering soil. A suitable sprig should have two to four nodes from which roots can develop. Soil preparation for sprigging is the same as for the other methods of planting.

To plant sprigs, dig furrows 8 to 12 inches apart and place the sprigs at a 1- to 2-inch depth (use the shallower depth if adequate moisture is available) 4 to 6 inches apart in the furrows. The closer the sprigs are, the faster the grass will cover the soil. After placing the sprigs in the furrow, cover a part of the sprig with soil and firm the soil around it. The foliage should be left exposed at the soil surface.

Another method is to place the sprigs on the soil surface at the desired interval end-to-end, about 6 inches apart, and then press one end of the sprig into the soil with a notched stick or a dull shovel. A portion of the sprig should be left aboveground exposed to light. Regardless of the planting method, each sprig should be tamped or rolled firmly into the soil. Water after planting. Since the sprigs are planted at a shallow depth, they are prone to drying out. Light, frequent waterings are necessary until roots become well established. Watering lightly once or twice daily will be required for several weeks after planting.

Care After Sprigging

It's extremely important to maintain a moist surface during the initial establishment from sprigs. If practical, topdress newly planted sprigs at regular intervals.

Plugging

The planting of 2- to 4-inch-diameter, circular or block-shaped pieces of sod at regular intervals is called plugging. Three to ten times as much planting material is necessary for plugging as for sprigging. The most common turfgrasses started by the use of plugs are St. Augustinegrass, zoysiagrass, and centipedegrass. Plugs are planted into prepared soil on 6- to 12-inch centers. The closer the plugs are planted together, the faster the sod will cover the area. However, the closer they are planted together, the more sod it will take to provide plugs to cover the lawn area.

Prior to plugging, prepare the soil the same as for seeding or sodding. Plugging can be done by machines designed to plant plugs, or by hand on smaller areas. Plug transplanting for warm-season turfgrasses should take place in the late spring or early summer. This will allow the turf the best chance to establish under choice growing conditions. After the plugs have been transplanted, the soil should be rolled to ensure good plant-to-soil contact. Irrigation should follow the same guidelines as for sodding.

Care After Plugging

Post-plugging care involves mowing at the height and frequency recommended for your particular turfgrass. Fertilizer applications made three to four weeks after plugging enhance the establishment rate. Proper irrigation procedures will also enhance establishment of a lawn through plugging.

Water as Needed

Common grasses will survive without watering except during the severest of droughts. If you want to maintain a green lawn in dry weather, add about 1 inch of water per week, preferably in the early morning, and only as much as will soak into the ground. To accurately measure the water you are applying, set a rain gauge within the sprinkler's locale. Water that is allowed to run off carries nutrients that are valuable to the lawn but harmful to the environment.

Unless you have bluegrass, it's safe to let an established lawn go dormant during dry periods. Dormancy is a survival mechanism and your lawn will usually recover when rainfall returns. Dormant lawns continue to protect water quality by holding soil and potential pollutants. Lightly sprinkling the turf can actually result in weaker plants.

Once you have an established lawn, water only when needed rather than on a schedule. Water if the grass develops a blue-gray color or when footprints are left on the turf after being walked on. Water slowly, preferably in the early morning. Wet the soil to a 4- to 6-inch depth. You can check the depth with a screwdriver. Shallow and infrequent watering, or watering in the evening, can damage your lawn. Do not allow water from a sprinkler or hose to run onto paved surfaces.

Chapter 4

FERTILIZATION

Fertilizer: *Any of a large number of natural and synthetic materials, including manure and nitrogen, phosphorus, and potassium compounds, spread on or worked into the soil to increase its fertility.*

A vital element in being able to display a spectacular mowing pattern is proper fertilization. A healthy, actively growing turfgrass plant will provide the perfect canvas on which to apply the design you've chosen. If a turfgrass plant is not supplied the correct levels of nutrients, it will become weakened and more susceptible to disease, weed infestation, and environmental stress. As a result, your time and effort in creating a pattern will not be diminished.

Plants require certain chemical elements for proper growth and appearance. Of these nutrients, at least 16 are known to be essential elements. All essential elements except carbon, hydrogen, and oxygen are obtained from the soil and absorbed by plant roots. If limited nutrients are available in the soil, lawn growth and quality may be limited. However, essential elements can be added to the soil through fertilizer applications.

Lawn fertilization is the application of sufficient amounts of all essential elements to produce optimum turf growth. These essential elements are of two types: macronutrients and micronutrients. Among the macronutrients, nitrogen, phosphorus, and potassium are required in the greatest quantities. These should be applied as recommended by soil test results. The macronutrients calcium, magnesium, and sulfur are needed in minor amounts, and are applied less frequently. These three elements are usually present in large enough quantities in the soil that they do not need to be added in a fertilizer. The micronutrients are iron, manganese, zinc, copper, molybdenum, chlorine, and boron. They are as essential as the macronutrients, but are required in much smaller amounts and are applied less often.

Understanding the nutritional requirements of the lawn and soil nutrient levels is perhaps the most important aspect of producing a quality stand of turfgrass. Fertilization of lawns is essential for the production of quality turf. However, exceeding recommended fertilizer application rates, or improper application timing, can pollute surface water and ground water quality. A well-planned and environmentally sound turfgrass fertilization program will take into account:

1. native soil fertility
2. nutrient source characteristics
3. desired turfgrass quality
4. nutrient application rate
5. application frequency
6. season of application
7. application method

A soil test is an excellent way to help determine the needs of the turf at your specific site. You should take a soil sample of your root zone and have it tested for Ph, nutrients, and the percentage of sand, silt, and clay in your mix.

Before purchasing any fertilizers there is important information to keep in mind. On every fertilizer label you will see three numbers. These stand for the nitrogen (N), phosphorus (P), and potassium (K) components, expressed in ratio form, by weight. For example, 21-10-10 would mean 21 parts of nitrogen to 10 parts of phosphorus and 10 parts of potassium.

Nitrogen is important for leaf and stem growth and provides the rich green color in a plant. It is the most important element you can apply that affects plant growth. Since nitrogen is a gas, it must be applied in the form of nitrogen compounds. A nitrogen fertility program should allow for slow, steady growth. Fertilizing with nitrogen levels that are too high will increase the incidence of diseases and thatch accumulation, and will make the turf more prone to winter damage. Several factors influence the nitrogen requirement of your lawn, including the species of grass being grown, the soil type, and the environmental conditions under which the turf is growing.

The second number in the ratio represents the amount of phosphorus, another major element needed for plant growth. It is supplied to the plant in the form of phosphate (P_2O_5). Phosphorus aids in germination and root growth. It's generally required in smaller amounts than either nitrogen or potassium, but plays a critical role in the establishment of turfgrasses. On soils that are low in phosphorus, a light application of this element will increase the growth rate during establishment. High levels of phosphorus can cause problems with turfgrass growth in grasses that are especially sensitive to high phosphorus levels, such as centipedegrass, so it's important to submit soil samples for nutrient analysis on a regular basis.

The third number represents the amount of potassium, which helps build plant tissue and aids in the production of chlorophyll. Potassium is supplied by potash (K_2O). Potassium is almost as important to turfgrass growth as nitrogen. It is critical for plant growth from the establishment phase through complete coverage. Adequate levels of potassium in the soil will allow the plant to withstand environmental and mechanical stresses. Most turfgrasses will better tolerate heat, cold, and drought situations when potassium levels are sufficient. Diseases become less of a problem too. Soil testing determines the level of potassium in the soil, and testing should be done regularly. Since potassium is leachable (i.e., it is washed out by water going down through the soil), fertilizers containing this element should be used on a regular basis.

An easy way to remember how N, P, and K affect the plant is up, down, and out. That is, N helps the leaves and upper parts of the plant grow, P helps the roots and germination, and K helps the plant spread and cover more area.

A fertilizer is said to be "complete" when it contains nitrogen, phosphorus, and potassium. Examples of commonly used fertilizers are 10-10-10, 16-16-16, and 20-10-5. An "incomplete" fertilizer will be missing one of the major components, and thus have only two numbers in its ratio.

The nitrate, phosphate, and potash in fertilizers are in the form of salts. It is these salts that are responsible for injuring the plants when one refers to "burning a yard" or "burning a field" after a fertilization application. It is important to carefully read the label of the product you're using. Don't use more than the recommended amounts of the fertilizer. It's not true that "if a little is good a lot must be better." If you apply too much, the salts in the formulation don't burn the turfgrass plant; instead, they suck the moisture out of the plant cells, desiccating (drying out) the plant. The salt index is a rating indicating the burn potential of that specific formulation, or how "hot" it is. Do not confuse it with the N-P-K numbers.

Safety

It's important to choose fertilizers wisely and apply them properly. When handling and applying turfgrass chemicals you must always think safety first. Each product will have specific guidelines pertaining to safety. Read the directions carefully to ensure your safety and to protect the environment.

Careful application of fertilizer can prevent pollution. Fertilizer applied to a healthy lawn at recommended rates normally will not contaminate surface or ground water. However, too much fertilizer applied is bad for the environment—not to mention a waste of money. Any chemical applied at too high a rate can build up to toxic levels and result in injury or death to the turf and also harm the ecosystem. The large areas of pavement in cities and suburbs provide a direct route for nutrients and pollutants to enter streams and rivers.

Follow these tips to make sure fertilizer remains on the lawn, stays out of the water, and doesn't pose a threat to the environment:

1. If your soil is sandy or if you live in an area with a high water table, use a slow-release nitrogen fertilizer and don't apply more than 1 pound of nitrogen per 1000 square feet in any individual application.
2. Keep fertilizer off paved surfaces. If granular fertilizer gets onto paved surfaces, collect it for later use or sweep it onto the lawn.
3. Use a drop spreader instead of a rotary spreader in restricted spaces, especially near water, driveways, or sidewalks.
4. Calibrate your spreader to make sure you're not overapplying fertilizer.
5. Fill and wash spreaders over grassy areas, not on hard surfaces.
6. Avoid getting fertilizer into natural drainage areas on your property. Be very careful when doing applications near lakes, ponds, streams, and rivers. Contamination of these bodies of water can affect the aquatic plants, fish and insects, and the chemical levels of the water.
7. Never apply fertilizer to frozen ground or dormant lawns. The runoff potential is too great. The unintentional migration of the

fertilizer will decrease effectiveness on the area you're treating and could contaminate the environment.

8. Don't use fertilizer to melt ice on sidewalks or driveways, and avoid ice-melting products that contain nitrogen.

9. Don't apply fertilizers in high winds. High winds will prevent the even distribution of the fertilizer, causing problems associated with too much material in some locations and not enough in others.

10. Be careful around children and pets. Check if the chemical has a reentry time before someone can go into the area without protective clothing.

11. Don't apply fertilizer in the heat of the day. Applications done at cooler temperatures will not put unnecessary stress on turf-grass plants.

12. Lightly water immediately following application in order to wash the fertilizer into the soil so that nutrients are available to the grass plants.

Effects of Overfertilizing

Too much fertilizer, or fertilizer applied at the wrong time, is detrimental to your lawn. Excess fertilizer causes rapid, lush growth, which is more susceptible to diseases and more attractive to pests. It's also important to apply fertilizer according to instructions at the proper time and rate to prevent water quality problems. Avoid getting fertilizer on sidewalks and driveways, where it can easily wash into storm drains and, eventually, into creeks, streams, and rivers. Nutrients, particularly nitrogen, cause water quality problems through leaching or runoff. (Leaching is the effect of nutrients being washed through the soil layers and into the ground water supply.) Leaching and runoff rob your soil of nutrients and lead to erosion. Plant ground cover in bare spots for prevention.

Fertilizer Timing

Because of their different growth cycles, proper timing of nitrogen applications is different for warm-season and cool-season turfgrasses. Excessive spring application of nitrogen to cool-season turf grasses, fescues, bluegrass, and ryegrass is detrimental because it leads to excessive leaf growth at the expense of stored food reserves and root growth. This increases the injury to lawns from summer diseases and drought. Late summer or early fall fertilizer applications are most beneficial to cool-season turfgrasses. This period is important for recovery from summer stresses. Late summer/early fall applications may reduce runoff and leaching potential because rainfall patterns, temperature, and plant growth rate tend to maximize nitrogen uptake. Apply the amounts of lime and fertilizer nutrients (nitrogen, phosphorus, and potassium) recommended in your soil test report. Application of fertilizers containing nitrogen should be made from September through December before freeze. By leaving grass clippings on the lawn, it is estimated that you can reduce nitrogen applications 20 percent to 30 percent after the first year and 35 percent to 45 percent after the second year.

The warm-season grasses—zoysiagrass and bermudagrass—should be fertilized in the early summer when they are most actively growing. Late summer and early fall applications of nitrogen to warm-season turfgrass without applying adequate amounts of phosphorus and potassium can increase winter injury.

Nitrogen Availability
The source of nitrogen in fertilizers influences nitrogen availability and turf response. There are two categories of nitrogen sources: quick-release and slow-release. Quick-release materials are water-soluble, can be readily used by the plant, are susceptible to leaching, and have a relatively short period of response. Quick-release sources include ammonium nitrate, urea, ammonium sulfate, and calcium nitrate.

Slow-Release Nitrogen Sources
The nitrogen in fertilizer can be in water-soluble or water-insoluble form. Slow-release nitrogen sources are fertilizers that have 40 percent or more of their nitrogen in water-insoluble forms. Slow-release fertilizers release nutrients over an extended period, are applied less frequently, and are applied at somewhat higher rates than the water-soluble nitrogen sources. The result is more uniform plant growth, less chance of injury to the grass, and less potential for nitrate leaching. Caution is needed when slow-release fertilizers are applied around trees or shrubs, as the later nutrient release may keep the plants growing into the fall when they should be hardening (going

dormant) for the winter. Slow-release fertilizers are a good choice for slopes, compacted soil, or sparsely covered lawns, because the potential for runoff and water contamination is less since the nutrients are released slowly.

If a fertilizer contains a slow-release nitrogen source, the portion of the nitrogen that is slowly available will be listed on the fertilizer bag as Water-Insoluble Nitrogen (WIN). If WIN is not listed on the fertilizer label, you should assume that it is all water-soluble or quickly available nitrogen. Products containing slow-release sources of nutrients usually have one or more of the following terms: water-insoluble, coated slow-release, slow-release, controlled release, slowly available water-soluble, or occluded slow-release. Sulfur-coated urea is a source of water-insoluble nitrogen. Urea nitrogen is a water-soluble source of nitrogen.

Your choices of slow-release nitrogen sources are:

- Natural organic materials made from manure, sewage sludge, Milorganite® 6-2-0 (made in Milwaukee, Wisconsin), or composted plant or animal products. The nitrogen content of these materials ranges from very low to around 10 percent.
- Sulfur-coated urea (SCU): 4-38 percent nitrogen
- Resin-coated urea: 24-35 percent nitrogen
- Isobutylidene diurea (IBDU): 30-31 percent nitrogen
- Ureaformaldehyde and methylene ureas: 20-38 percent Nitrogen

Determining the Percentage of WIN (Water-Insoluble Nitrogen)

A fertilizer label may supply the following information:

20-10-10
Guaranteed analysis
Total nitrogen   20 percent
Water-insoluble nitrogen   8 percent
Available phosphates   10 percent
Water-soluble potash   10 percent

To calculate the percentage of WIN, divide the percentage of water-insoluble nitrogen by the percentage of total nitrogen and multiply by 100. In this case, the result is 8 percent divided by 20 percent x 100 = 40 percent. This fertilizer contains 40 percent WIN, and is therefore considered a slow-release nitrogen source.

Fertilizer Application

Most fertilizers are applied at a rate determined by the type and amount of nitrogen present in the material. Nitrogen is the nutrient most used by grass and is often the element that burns the lawn if applied at excessive rates. An almost universal recommendation for turfgrasses is to apply 1 pound of actual nitrogen per 1,000 square feet of lawn area if more than one-half (50 percent) of the nitrogen (N) is quick-release or from a water-soluble source. If most (greater than 50 percent) of the nitrogen in the fertilizer is water-insoluble, then the rate may be 2 pounds of actual N per 1,000 square feet.

The pounds of actual nitrogen in every fertilizer can be determined by dividing 100 by the percent N listed on the label. For example, in applying soluble nitrogen from ammonium sulfate, divide 100 by 20 (the nitrogen percentage of ammonium sulfate) to find out the number of pounds of fertilizer that will supply 1 pound of N. Since 100 divided by 20 equals 5, apply 5 pounds of ammonium sulfate per 1,000 square feet of lawn. If you are applying N in a 16-4-8 fertilizer and the nitrogen in the product is all slow-release nitrogen, you could apply 2 pounds of actual nitrogen. The calculation is the same as in the first example. Divide 100 by 16 (16 is the percent N in the fertilizer). The answer is about 6, so 12 pounds of the 16-4-8 fertilizer would supply 2 pounds of nitrogen.

Soil Type

Sandy soils will generally leach more nitrogen than silt-loam and clay-loam soils. Therefore, more frequent nitrogen applications are often required in sandy soils when quick-release sources of nitrogen are used. Using slow-release fertilizers can minimize leaching, which in turn can reduce the problem of nitrogen-enriched water in nearby streams and lakes.

Type and Age of Turfgrass

Nitrogen application to cool-season grasses, such as tall fescue, is best done in late summer and fall. Warm-season grasses perform best when nitrogen is applied in mid-spring to mid-summer. Newly established lawns or lawns lacking density or ground cover will benefit from properly timed applications of nitrogen until ground cover and density have reached a desirable level. A mature centipedegrass and carpetgrass lawn will require lower levels of nitrogen than other warm-season grasses.

Length of Growing Season
A turfgrass growing in an area with a longer growing season will require more nitrogen.

Traffic
Where heavy traffic or use is anticipated, higher rates of suitably timed nitrogen and potassium can help the grass recuperate and recover from injury.

Shade
Grasses growing in heavily shaded areas require only one-half to two-thirds as much nitrogen as grasses growing in full sun. Reducing the amount of nitrogen to grasses growing in the shade reduces the incidence of disease. For heavily shaded cool-season grasses, time your fertilizer application after the majority of leaves have fallen from the trees in the fall, since grass plants can best use nitrogen when sunlight can reach the grass leaves.

Quality Desired
Turfgrass quality is a measure of density, color, uniformity (freedom from weeds and undesired grasses), smoothness, growth habit, and texture. If above-average or superior levels of turfgrass quality are desired, a commitment must be made to proper turfgrass species, cultivar selection, frequent mowing, and slightly higher rates of nitrogen and application frequency. In addition, irrigation, aerification, and pesticide application may at times enhance quality.

Micronutrients
Fertilizers that contain micronutrients should be applied if a deficiency exists. This can be determined through soil and tissue testing. Sometimes warm-season grasses such as centipedegrass and St. Augustinegrass turn yellow during the summer because of a lack of nitrogen fertilizer. However, overfertilizing with nitrogen in summer is not desirable since it encourages disease and insect problems.

Two micronutrients that can influence the appearance of turfgrass plants are iron (Fe) and manganese (Mn). If applied the week before a big game, tournament, party, or event they will add more depth to the pattern on the turf. The addition of iron to these grasses often provides the desirable dark green color but does not stimulate the excessive grass growth that nitrogen fertilization does. Usually iron sulfate (2 ounces per 3 to 5 gallons of water per 1,000 square feet) or a chelated iron source is used to provide this greening effect. Deeper color can make a significant impact on the contrast of the light and dark green stripes in a pattern, resulting in improved aesthetics of your designs. Supplemental iron (Fe) and manganese (Mn) can be applied by means of liquid or granular applications. Products comprised of chelated iron forms will provide a quicker response. The drastic color enhancement results are only temporary, however, so repeat applications are necessary.

A wide range of iron and manganese products are available from many different companies. I have had good response from P.B.I. Gordon's Ferro Mec® liquid iron product. The greening effect of a liquid product can usually be seen within 48 hours of application. I have seen wonderful results from the granular micronutrient package product STEP® by The O.M. Scott Company. Among its ingredients are both Fe and Mn. When watered in thoroughly at the recommended rate, greening can be seen in approximately 72 hours, depending on the weather and the soil mix. Both of these are important parts of the fertilization program at Milwaukee County Stadium for the Kentucky bluegrass/perennial ryegrass mix. They can be used as a turfgrass management tool to provide a dark green turf to showcase your patterns.

Be careful when handling and applying iron products. They can stain clothing, concrete, bricks, and pavement. Remove or wash away any extra spray or overspread products from your application to prevent the possibility of stains.

A determining factor in any iron application should be concern over frost. If you apply an iron product and it frosts within 24 hours, you may see the turf you were hoping to green up turn black. The risk far outweighs any temporary benefit, so it is better to reschedule your application if any chance of frost exists. It is better to be safe than sorry.

Fertilizer Application Equipment and Methods

Fertilizers can be applied in either a dry or a liquid formulation. It's extremely important to achieve a uniform application. Uneven applications will cause an uneven greening in the lawn. Uniform applications will eliminate streaks of different shades of green turf in the lawn. Excessive application of a fertilizer may also cause burning of the turfgrass, leaving brown or even dead areas. Proper application of nitrogen fertilizers by hand is difficult even for a trained professional. Spreaders should be used.

There are two basic types of fertilizer spreaders available for use on the home lawn. The drop spreader "drops" the fertilizer through a series of openings at the base of the hopper. This type is best suited for fertilizing small areas or when trying to prevent fertilizer from getting on sidewalks or paved surfaces. The amount of fertilizer that is spread depends on the opening setting, the type of fertilizer used, and the speed at which the spreader is pushed. When using a drop spreader it's important to overlap the wheel tracks because all of the fertilizer is distributed between the wheels. Drop spreaders are not as easy to maneuver around trees and shrubs as are rotary spreaders. They are well suited for making applications near bodies of water, in order to minimize contamination.

Home lawn misapplication of fertilizer. This did produce a striping pattern but it is not recommended. Nor is it as pretty as the patterns you can create using the techniques in this book. Photo courtesy of Wayne Horman, the O.M. Scotts Company.

Broadcast spreaders, also called rotary or cyclone spreaders, have a rotating disc that "throws out" fertilizer in a semicircular pattern as they are pushed. This type of spreader is best suited for covering large areas quickly. The distribution pattern is not uniform, but by controlling the overlap you can get good uniformity. Rotary spreaders usually give better distribution where sharp turns are encountered, such as around trees and shrubs. Apply one-half of the fertilizer in one direction and the other half at a right angle to minimize streaking.

Calibrate Your Spreader

Spreader instructions and fertilizer labels may supply recommended settings for various application rates. If the information is not provided, you will have to calibrate your spreader to ensure proper application. Once you have calibrated for a particular product, mark the setting on your spreader or on the product bag so you will have it for the next application.

Calibrating a Drop Spreader

Following are directions for calibrating a drop spreader.

1. Measure the width of your spreader.
2. Mark off the distance needed to make the spreader cover 100 square feet. For example, if your spreader is 2 feet wide, the distance is 50 feet. For 1-foot and 3-foot spreaders, the distances are 66⅔ and 33⅓ feet, respectively.
3. Attach a catch pan to the spreader. A piece of cardboard folded into a V shape works well.
4. Set the spreader to a low setting.
5. Make sure the hopper is closed, then fill it with a few pounds of the fertilizer you intend to spread.
6. Starting 10 feet behind the 100-square-foot test area, push the spreader forward and open the hopper as you reach the starting point. Close the hopper as you go over the finish line.
7. Weigh the collected fertilizer and multiply by 10. The result is the amount of fertilizer that would be spread per 1000 square feet at that spreader setting or calibration.
8. Compare the result with your target application rate and adjust if necessary to deliver more or less fertilizer.

9. Repeat Steps 5-8 until you reach the desired application rate. You can run the test on a paved surface. If you do, make sure you sweep up as much of the fertilizer as possible.

Example for a drop spreader using fertilizer that is 20 percent nitrogen:

a. Spreader width is 2 feet.
b. Mark off 50 feet to get a 100-square-foot test area.
c. At Step 7 you find you dispensed H pound of material.
d. Multiply this number by 10 to get the application per 1000 square feet: H x 10 = 5.

The application rate is 5 pounds of fertilizer per 1000 square feet. This would supply one pound of nitrogen (5 pounds of material x 20 percent nitrogen 1 pound of nitrogen).

To avoid missing parts of the lawn and to obtain a uniform application, calibrate your spreader to deliver ½ of the desired rate, then cover the lawn twice. Make the first application in one direction and the second application at a right angle to the first.

Calibrating a Rotary Spreader

Following are directions for calibrating a rotary spreader.

1. Fill the spreader with a few pounds of the fertilizer.
2. Measure the width of the application. It is helpful to have a second person watch and mark how far the fertilizer is thrown to the sides of the spreader.
3. Empty the hopper.
4. Measure a distance that when multiplied by the width of application from Step 2 results in 1000. For example, if the application width is 10 feet (5 on each side of the spreader), mark off a 100-foot strip (10 x 100 = 1000).
5. Fill the hopper with a known weight of material.
6. Begin 10 feet behind the starting line. Push the spreader forward and open the hopper as your reach the starting line. Close the hopper as you go over the finish line.
7. Empty the remaining fertilizer onto a plastic sheet, then transfer it to a bucket and weigh it.

8. Subtract the weight found in Step 7 from the starting weight in Step 5. The result is the amount of fertilizer dispensed per 1000 square feet.
9. Compare this rate with the target application rate, and adjust the setting to deliver more or less as necessary.
10. Repeat Steps 4-9 until the desired rate is achieved.

Example for a rotary spreader using fertilizer that is 33 percent nitrogen:

a. The application width is 8 feet (4 feet on each side).
b. Place 5 pounds of material in the hopper.
c. Divide 1000 by 8 (the application width) to find the length of test area needed to get 1000 square feet (1000 divided by 8 = 125). 125 feet x the 8-foot application width = 1000 square feet.
d. After making one pass with the spreader, weigh the material left in the hopper and you will find 2 pounds. When you subtract 2 pounds from the starting weight of 5 pounds, you will find that 3 pounds were dispensed. The application rate is 3 pounds of material per 1000 square feet. This would supply 1 pound of nitrogen (3 pounds of material x 33 percent nitrogen = 1 pound of nitrogen).

Used appropriately, fertilizers are an important turfgrass management component. Always follow label directions for application, handling, and storage instructions.

Chapter 5

COMMON NUISANCES

Weed: *an unwanted plant.* This definition could fit any type of plant. A beautiful rose bush could be considered a weed if it were growing in the middle of a baseball field. I do have lush green grass in my home lawn, but it is also spotted with dandelions because my daughters love to make necklaces and pick bouquets of them. They made me stop one day and take a close look at the bloom, extolling its beauty for it's many curled stamens and lustrous color. I had to agree with them. At our house the seedheads are better known as "blow flowers" because Victoria loves to puff on them, scattering the seeds. Her cultural practices lead me to believe we will never run out of the bright yellow blossoms.

Crabgrass Control

Crabgrass is a major lawn weed. It belongs to a group of weeds called annual grasses. The information in this section on controlling crabgrass applies to foxtail, goosegrass, and barnyardgrass as well.

An understanding of the growth cycle of annual grasses is important in developing control strategies. The seed deposited on the ground from the previous fall will germinate from mid-spring through mid-summer. Germination is dependent on soil temperature, not air temperature. The individual plants establish and spread quickly during the summer months. Each annual grass plant produces thousands of seeds from mid-summer through early fall, until it is killed by the first frost.

There are several nonherbicidal control approaches to consider in reducing a crabgrass infestation in a lawn.

Nonherbicidal Control

Mow as high as practical during the summer months for the grass species present in your lawn. Bluegrass, tall fescue, fine fescue, and ryegrass should be maintained at 3 inches during the summer. Crabgrass seed requires high light intensity to germinate, and the shaded environment near the soil surface in a high-mown lawn helps deter seed germination. The higher mowing height also produces a healthier grass plant. A low mowing height encourages weeds such as crabgrass.

Mow at intervals frequent enough so that no more than one-third of the grass blade is removed in one mowing. Letting a turf grow tall and then cutting it back to a low height will cause a reduction in turf density, resulting in voids where crabgrass can grow.

Irrigate properly to help reduce crabgrass infestation. In the absence of rainfall, water once or twice per week and wet the soil profile to a depth of 6 inches. Lighter, more frequent irrigations can encourage crabgrass seed germination.

Fertilize at least once per year. A good program consists of a September fertilization followed by a second fertilization in early November.

Herbicidal Control

Pre-Emergent Herbicides

Pre-emergent herbicides control crabgrass by preventing establishment of seedling crabgrass. To be effective, pre-emergent herbicides must be applied before the crabgrass seed germinates. A general guide for when to spray a pre-emergent herbicide is to spray when the forsythia is blooming in your area. Remember that the germination of crabgrass will vary from year to year depending on the weather. Crabgrass germination is favored by periods of rainfall and warm nights rather than by specific calendar dates. A pre-emergent herbicide will not control crabgrass after the crabgrass seed has germinated and formed leaves above the turf canopy.

The pre-emergent herbicide must be applied uniformly across the lawn to establish a chemical barrier and achieve a successful crabgrass control program. This way the crabgrass will not move from one area of the lawn to another.

Pre-emergent herbicides biodegrade, or break down, during the summer months. The length of time a given pre-emergent herbicide will be effective against crabgrass cannot be accurately predicted. The breakdown is controlled in part by weather conditions. As a result, weather patterns that favor a faster than normal breakdown of a pre-emergent herbicide can lead to a lawn infested with late-germinating annual grass, such as crabgrass.

Under normal weather patterns, pre-emergent herbicides will give 90 to 95% control. To maximize control, consider the following guidelines. Always read the pesticide label for detailed information before using any product.

Do not use pre-emergent herbicides at the time of seeding except for products containing Siduron®, considered a selective pre-emergent. Siduron®—containing pre-emergents will control crabgrass yet allow Kentucky bluegrass to germinate. Careful timing must be used and product label instructions must be followed for the herbicide to be effective. Otherwise the grass seed you are planting will not germinate. In general, wait until the new grass has been mowed three times before applying a pre-emergent herbicide.

After a pre-emergent herbicide is applied, wait two to four months before seeding, depending on the product used. Refer to the label for the length of time to wait before seeding.

If sod is laid, do not apply pre-emergent herbicides to the soil. The pre-emergent chemical may inhibit rooting. If it does not rain within one week of application, apply adequate water (½ inch) to wash the chemical off the grass and onto the soil surface. Some herbicides require immediate watering-in. Refer to the pesticide label for specific instructions.

Do not dethatch or vigorously cultivate the surface after the pre-emergent application. The chemical barrier could be disturbed, significantly reducing the percentage of weed control.

Pre-emergent herbicides do not control nutsedge (nutgrass) or perennial broadleaf weeds, such as dandelion. Some herbicides will reduce a few of the summer annuals (spurge). Again, read the label for detailed information.

Post-Emergent Herbicides

Post-emergent herbicides can be used on crabgrass, foxtail, and barnyardgrass after they have germinated. Before using post-emergent herbicides consider the following.

Post-emergent herbicides may cause a temporary discoloration of the turf. If the soil is dry, water the turf to a 6-inch depth the day before the treatment. During hot, dry weather apply an additional ½ inch of water two days after application.

Mix and apply post-emergent herbicides according to label directions. A yellowing of the crabgrass is evidence of control. Overapplication will cause sudden browning of the turf. If overapplication does occur, irrigate the treated area with 1 inch of water as soon as possible. Repeat the irrigation in five days.

With late summer or early fall treatment it's best to wait two weeks before reseeding the treated area.

Post-emergent crabgrass herbicides should not be applied to a newly seeded lawn until it has been mowed at least three times.

Medium to mature crabgrass may require a second application of post-emergent herbicide four to seven days after the initial application. Irrigate the turf with 1 inch of water two days after the second treatment to minimize damage.

Herbicides should be applied when air temperatures range from 70 to 85°F. Shade or cloudy weather, accompanied by cooler temperatures, decreases the effectiveness of these products.

The above are general guidelines. Always read and follow the label for each herbicide before using it. Follow the label recommendation when a discrepancy occurs. If crabgrass occupies a majority of the lawn consider a total renovation of the lawn in the fall.

Think Outside the Box

In the early 1990s a friend who is a university turfgrass professor stopped by the stadium in Milwaukee to see me while he was in town. During his visit I asked if he could identify a few trouble spots on the baseball field. There were four or five small spots on the foul area grass near the warning track. These areas exhibited disease signs of a frogeye pattern (a dead spot in the middle of a circle surrounded by darker green grass at the edges of the spot).

He knelt down and closely examined the spots. Several minutes passed as he ruled out possibilities, but did not diagnose the cause. I don't believe he ever considered the chance that an animal had caused the damage. Why would he? We were on a Major League Baseball field confined within a stadium. If I had not seen it with my own eyes I would never have figured it out. A week earlier I had seen a wild cat run from the dugout, across the warning track, and onto the foul area grass. It urinated, then ran back into the dugout, up the runway, and into the basement of the stadium. The spots were caused by the concentrated location of the cat urine in the soil. I revealed the cause of the spots to the professor. I still chuckle when I think of that day, and I assume he does too.

Dog Spot Disease

The Turf Resource Center (TRC) asked Dr. Steve Thompson, DVM director, Purdue University Veterinary Teaching Hospital, to explain why animal wastes affect grass the way they do. Dr. Thompson concluded that it was not the pH in the dog urine but the concentration of nitrogen that caused turf damage. Nitrogen is removed from the animal's body by the kidneys as a waste product, resulting from the breakdown of proteins. Urine is more damaging to turfgrass than feces because it is applied all at once, where as feces dissolve slowly, allowing for removal. With dogs, the males mark their territory while lifting their leg, using several small-volume sprays, while females squat and urinate in puddles, concentrating the nitrogen effect.

Controlling Damage

The best way to control dog damage to lawns is to control where the dog eliminates. Walk the dog on a leash and guide it to a designated area, possibly mulched, with a marking post, boulder, or even faux fire hydrant. Dietary supplements used to change the pH of the dog's urine are not recommended. Ascorbic acid (vitamin C), fruit juices, baking soda, and other supplements can be harmful to dogs. Since the urine pH is not the cause of the turf damage, dietary supplements are of no benefit.

A motion-activated sprinkler, new on the market, may be of benefit in keeping animals off your turf. Designed to scare cats and rabbits from gardens, it could work in small yards or corners where damage frequently occurs. Even if it does not scare the animal away, the added water will dilute the nitrogen concentration, decreasing the burn effect. If animals or children continually activate your sprinkler, it could cause overwatering and high water bills.

If a dog does urinate on your turfgrass, flush the area with water to dilute the nitrogen concentration. Watering the area any time up to eight hours after the dog urinates will result in a fertilizer effect rather than a burn. Waiting longer increases the chance and severity of the burning action.

Chapter 6

MOWING RECOMMENDATIONS

Finding the right balance between turf and human needs requires planning and consideration. Mowing practices—including mowing height, mowing frequency, and handling clippings—require primary consideration. Mowing is the most time-consuming of all turf maintenance activities. We generally mow turfgrasses for two reasons. The main reason is to improve turfgrass appearance. Mowing turf at appropriate heights and frequencies is the most important component of a turf management plan designed to develop dense, actively growing, attractive turf. Another reason for mowing turfgrasses is to produce recreational or sports playing surfaces. Many outdoor athletic or play activities—such as golf, tennis, lawn bowling, baseball, soccer, and football—take place on turf surfaces specifically mowed and managed to accommodate them.

Turfgrasses are well adapted to frequent mowing, but mowing too short will reduce the vigor of the plant by reducing its ability to manufacture food. There is a direct relationship between cutting height and the root mass that a grass plant can maintain. As the height is lowered, the root system is reduced. This restricts the ability of the plant to take up water and nutrients. At higher cuts, lawn grasses are more stress-tolerant, which is especially important during the summer heat period. Taller grass plants with higher density have a profound shading effect on the soil surface, reducing weed seed germination, particularly of crabgrass. This is an excellent way to reduce herbicide use.

Mowing Height

Although recommended cutting heights vary by type of grass, a good guideline is the "one-third rule." This rule states that you should never cut off more than one-third of the grass plant at any one mowing.

Removing more than one-third of total leaf surface can severely shock the grass plant by decreasing its ability to support root growth. Root growth ceases while the leaves and shoots are regrowing. Roots may not fully develop and the grass plants will be more susceptible to environmental and management stresses.

Low mowing is a major cause of lawn deterioration. This practice can be especially destructive if repeated over successive mowings. Maintenance of healthy turf root systems should be a primary consideration of any turf management program.

Mow turfgrasses according to the heights presented in *Table 1*. Note that a range is listed for each species. When healthy and actively growing, turf can be mowed at the lower range. Raise mowing heights within the desired range during warm or hot periods or when turf is stressed due to drought, disease, shade, insects, or traffic. The heights listed in this table provide a balance between turf appearance and health.

Table 1. Mowing Heights for Different Grasses

Tall fescue (*Festuca arundinacea*)	2.5-3.5 in.
Perennial ryegrass (*Lolium perenne*)	2-3 in.
Kentucky bluegrass (*Poa pratensis*)	2-3 in.
Fine fescue (*Festuca rubra*)	2.5-3.5 in.
Bermudagrass (*Cynodon dactylon*)	0.5-1 in.
Zoysiagrass (*Zoysia species*)	0.5-1.5 in.
Creeping bentgrass (*Agrostis stolonifera*)	0.25-0.75 in.
Buffalograss (*Buchloe dactyloides*)	2-3 in.

When to Mow

Turf should be mowed as necessary, not according to a preset schedule. Turfgrass growth rates depend on weather, management, and species. For best results, use the one-third rule described earlier. For example, Kentucky bluegrass being maintained at a 2-inch height should be mowed when it reaches 3 inches. Maintaining your turf at the recommended height may require mowing twice a week in the spring, every other week in the summer, and once a week in the fall. Infrequent mowing is a major cause of lawn deterioration. Frequent mowing will encourage deeper roots—which are important to the turf's health as temperatures rise in summer—and will etch in pattern lines.

Table 2 illustrates the desired height of cut and the growth allowed between mowings according to the one-third rule. As the table illustrates, higher cutting heights allow more time between mowing cycles, which can be advantageous during periods of rapid growth. For example, to maintain a 3-inch height, do not let the grass get much taller than 4 inches. Mowing to the proper height can reduce weed problems by as much as 50 to 80 percent.

Table 2. When to Mow to Cut One-Third of the Leaf Blade

Desired Height	Mow When Turf Reaches	Growth Between Mowings
1.0	1.5 in.	0.5 in.
2.0 in.	3.0 in.	1.0 in.
2.5 in.	3.75 in.	1.25 in.
3.0 in.	4.5 in.	1.5 in.
3.5 in.	5.25 in.	1.75 in.

The turfgrass species and the use of the turf are the most important factors to consider when selecting the height of cut. Kentucky bluegrass and perennial ryegrass will tolerate the lower end of the range, while tall fescue and fine fescue will benefit from the higher end of the range. Shaded turfs should be mowed at the high end of the range to maximize leaf surface area.

Mow Regularly

Proper height and frequency are the two most important aspects of a turf mowing program. By mowing frequently and maintaining a uniform turf surface, a neat appearance can be achieved, even at taller heights. Unfortunately, a common perception is that a short turf is superior in appearance to tall turf. In reality, turf that is uniform appears neater than uneven turf, regardless of height.

Other Recommendations

Occasionally, personal schedules or weather conditions prevent turf mowing when it's needed. If this occurs, mow using the one-third rule. If the turf is 6 inches tall, and the desired height is 2 inches, the first mowing should be at 4 inches, or at the highest setting close to 4 inches. Several days later, mow again, reducing the mowing height using the one-third rule. This mowing should be lower than 4 inches. Continue this pattern until the turf is adjusted to the proper height.

Two other mowing recommendations are to maintain mower blade sharpness, and to mow when grass is dry. Dull blades tear turf leaves, leaving a ragged appearance. Ragged leaf edges contribute to turf water loss and increased incidence of turf diseases. Cleanly cut turf looks better and is often healthier than turf with torn leaves. Mow when turf is dry. Wet turf can clog the mower and form clumpy masses on the turf surface.

Scalping

When turf is cut excessively short, scalping can also occur. Scalping can happen as a result of irregular land contours, excessive thatch, infrequent mowing, or poor mower adjustment. Scalped turf appears brown and stubbly due to the removal of healthy leaves and exposure of turf crowns, dead leaves, or even the bare soil. Avoid scalping turf, as it is unattractive, and in some cases, severely scalped turf may not recover. When you purchase your next mower, look for one featuring a floating deck or reel unit that will follow the contours of the ground to prevent scalping.

Mowing Direction

Frequent and close mowing in one direction or pattern can cause turf shoots to lean in the direction of the cut, causing a grain to develop. On closely clipped turf, such as a golf course putting green, grain is undesirable because it can alter the path of a putted ball. If you alter the mowing pattern, turf shoots will tend to grow more upright, which reduces grain. In addition, altering the mowing pattern can reduce excessive wear from your wheels or rollers always traveling the same route. In general, alter the mowing pattern every two to three weeks. In small gardens or sloping areas, use the most convenient or safest mowing pattern at each mowing.

Turf managers at athletic fields, homeowners, and landscape contractors are using mowing patterns to provide visual interest for their turf. These patterns are setting a high standard throughout the turf industry. These turfs are mowed frequently in the same direction for two to three weeks at a time using reel mowers or rotary mowers with rollers attached to provide head-turning patterns. (Look to Chapter 14, Pattern Instructions, for easy-to-follow step-by-step examples on creating patterns.)

First and Last Mowing of the Season

The first and last mowing of the year are sometimes handled differently than others. In spring before the grass begins to grow, mow the turf slightly shorter than normal but still in the range shown in *Table 1* to remove dead blades and other debris. Be careful not to scalp turf during this initial mowing. Once turf begins active growth, mow at the proper height and frequency. The last mowing of the year should be at the normal mowing height. Turf should neither be cut excessively short nor be allowed to become excessively long going into winter.

Retaining Grass Clippings

Return clippings to the lawn whenever possible. Bagging grass clippings and discarding them with the trash robs your lawn of important nutrients. Also, recent legislation in many states prohibits residents from dumping yard wastes like grass clippings and leaves at landfills.

In order for the lawn to benefit from retaining clippings, the lawn should be mowed with less than one-third of the total leaf length removed. The resulting small leaf portions readily filter down to the soil surface and decompose easily. (Clippings larger than one-third of the leaf length cannot filter down, and therefore they accumulate on the surface.)

When clippings are returned a small quantity of organic matter and large quantities of mineral nutrients are returned to the soil, contributing to improved soil conditions. *Table 3* shows the fertilizer content of clippings. If the total does not seem substantial, keep in mind that clippings are approximately 90% water by weight. The benefits of returning clippings can occur quickly. When returned into a healthy turfgrass environment, clippings were found to release nutrients into soil in as little as fourteen days.

Table 3. Fertilizer Content of Typical Grass Clippings

Nutrient	(Content by Weight)
Nitrogen	4%
Potassium	2%
Phosphorus	0.5%

Returning clippings to the turf also has several other benefits. It eliminates the need for disposal in landfills and reduces the time and energy required to transport clippings to composting facilities. When clippings are returned to the turf, the consumer does not bear the cost of commercial composting.

Leaving grass clippings on the lawn reduces the amount of fertilizer needed for a healthy lawn.

Not collecting clippings saves time and expense. Emptying grass catchers does not interrupt mowing. A Colorado study found that 1,000 square feet of highly fertilized Kentucky bluegrass yielded 529 pounds of clippings in one year. If clippings were collected, work stoppage would occur 22 times to empty a basket that accommodated 25 pounds of clippings.

By following these guidelines on returning clippings, homeowners can expect to save money on fertilizer and plastic trash bags. Annual homeowner savings for a typical quarter-acre lot amount to $20 to $45 in fertilizer costs and $20 to $40 for trash bags. In addition, you will help your local government keep a lid on refuse disposal costs. A typical quarter-acre lot generates 3,500 to 4,000 pounds of grass clippings per year. Disposing of them costs the homeowner $50 to $90 a year in public service charges, private collector fees, or taxes.

Removing Clippings

Excessive accumulations of clippings, a result of infrequent mowing, may smother the turf and should be removed. During the peak growing periods, in April or May, it may be necessary because of sheer volume to collect grass clippings.

Many gardeners use clippings as mulch in vegetable or ornamental gardens. This is an excellent use, but precautions should be taken when using clippings shortly after weed control products have been applied to the turf. In tests conducted at Michigan State University, researchers applied several pest control products to lawn turf, then mowed at 2-day and 14-day intervals after application. The clippings were used as mulch around a variety of annual flowers and vegetable plants. Some weed control products that had been applied to the turf caused injury to the flowers and vegetables when clippings were used as mulch up to 14 days after application. Insect or disease control products had no effect on the flowers and vegetables. The conclusion: Allow at least three mowings after application of weed control products before using clippings as mulch. Clippings from the first three mowings can be returned to the soil or composted. Weed control products will degrade quickly during the compost process and won't harm the system.

When to Collect Clippings

There are five situations where clipping collection is recommended.

- When clippings are long and thick.
- When clippings interfere with the use of the turf or surrounding area.
- When the potential for disease development is increased by returning clippings.
- When the mowing equipment in use necessitates collection.
- To recycle later in the day to hide aesthetically unpleasant spots on the turf. *(See Chapter 10, Techniques to Help Hide Damaged Turf, for tips on how to do this.)*

Unless one of these situations is encountered, returning clippings is recommended.

There are several ways of dealing with clippings if they are still visible on the turf surface 24 hours after mowing. By removing the turf, the clippings will be recut and reduced in size. This will also redistribute the smaller clippings and allow them to filter to the ground. Another way to move and disperse clippings is by waving a long pole or garden hose through clumps of clippings.

In summary, mow frequently at the recommended height using the "one-third rule." Maintain blade sharpness, mow when turf is dry, and return clippings to produce the healthiest and best quality turf possible.

Clippings and Thatch

Clippings are often thought to contribute to thatch buildup. This only happens when excessively long clippings are returned to turf. Thatch is primarily composed of turfgrass roots, crowns, rhizomes, sheaths, and stolons. These plant parts contain large amounts of lignin, a waxy substance that decomposes slowly. Turf clippings, on the other hand, contain little lignin and are usually composed of at least 75% to 85% water. After drying, short clippings break down quickly. Clippings may, however, contribute to thatch when tall grass is mowed too short, resulting in large clippings. Mowing at proper intervals ensures small clipping size and rapid clipping breakdown.

Chapter 7

MAKING TURNS WITH YOUR MOWER

Making turns with the mower may seem like quite a simple operation, but there are actually several techniques you can take advantage of to avoid damaging the turf surface and enhance the overall appearance.

Take care when making turns on grass surfaces so that the tread on the tires does not tear or injure the turfgrass plants. If you turn too fast or make too tight of a turn the tire friction can cause damage.

To prevent harming your grass, learn how to make turns properly on a riding mower. The proper turn is similar to the "Y" turn learned in driver education classes. Before starting your turn it is usually best to raise the cutting reels or mowing deck to prevent the rollers from rolling back and forth on the grass, adding wear or unwanted lines. Most turning marks can be removed when you perform the last step in your design—the cleanup passes, framing in your masterpiece.

When making a 180-degree turn on the grass surface mow almost to the end of your line. Stop, back up slowly to allow room for an unhurried wide turn (similar to a teardrop shape), and pull up beside the previous mowing line. Then carefully back up and align the mower with the edge of the prior stripe.

Be sure the blades or reels of the mower are disengaged and not down on the turf when you're setting up your final alignment for the next stripe. If you have the blades or reels engaged and lowered onto the grass when you're stopped, the high-speed turning action of the cutting blades will hurt the grass. A reel mower will leave whitish-brown stripes the width of each reel on the grass and a rotary mower will leave a circular shape on the grass where you stop. This whitish-brown appearance is caused by the frayed grass blade tips, which are caused by the repeated spinning of the blades in one spot. Do not engage the blades until you're ready to move forward. It's important to be sure that you're starting off straight. If you're not sure, pull forward far enough to enable you to back up and realign the mower or a little bend in the line will start, getting bigger with each subsequent line you create.

By making a slow, wide turn, you can avoid turning damage to the turf caused by the tire tread. You will eliminate the chance of turning too sharply and you won't have to worry about the tire marks you are making because you are turning on the area where future lines will wipe away any noticeable tire marks. Any remaining visible markings can be removed when you do your final cleanup passes and frame in your pattern. Remember that you can adjust the number of cleanup passes to whatever works best for your situation.

While the deck or reels are raised it's important not to turn too quickly because any clippings in the grass baskets—or that have collected on top of the reels—can spill off during a fast turn and leave an unsightly mess. The deck or reels may also tilt and gouge the turf. I've operated some mowers that, when operated carefully, will allow the deck to be left down when making turns. There are many different manufacturers of mowers and each mower will operate a little differently. With practice on your own machine, you will find what works best for you.

The tires on the side you're turning into tend to grab most with any mower. Watch that side's tire or tires for the first signs of damage. Another way to prevent turf damage is to change the tires on your mower to a tire with a smoother surface. If the site you are mowing is relatively flat the extra tread on fairway reel mowers or even lawn tractors is not needed. *Only switch to smooth tires if it is not going to affect the traction needed for mowing safety at your particular site.* At Milwaukee County Milwaukee Stadium we changed the three standard tires that came with our triplex reel mower to three smoother tires that are ribbed, almost slick. Since we are mowing the baseball field we don't need deep tread for traction safety. By switching to a smoother, ribbed tire we eliminated worry about the tire tread grabbing and tearing the plant or grass blades when turning.

On a triplex reel mower you need to think of the back tire when trying to prevent damage. Be careful not to turn the steering wheel quickly because that back tire can also harm the turfgrass by grabbing. On a lawn tractor or landscape mower be aware of the size of the tread on your tires and how you are turning. Many sites require a larger tread for safety. In these cases you must make slow, wide, careful turns.

Damage from turns can happen on all types of turf. The higher the moisture level in the soil the easier it is to cause damage, so be extra careful. At higher moisture levels the plant material is tender and the growing medium is more apt to shift, cutting the roots of the plant. For your own safety and the health of the grass: **Do not mow when the grass is wet unless you absolutely must and then be very careful.**

Evaluate your site and determine if it's possible to turn the mower around on a warning track, baseline, driveway, or sidewalk. This can alleviate the problem of tire marks and damage to the turf. Make sure you don't track material from those areas back onto the grass. When making turns on a driveway, sidewalk, baseline, or warning track, take precaution before lowering the mower deck or reels to be sure you are entirely on the grass. Lowering them too soon will cause wear problems along the edge, detracting from the manicured look you're striving for. Since easy turnaround areas are not always available on site it's important to learn how to turn your mower around on a turfgrass surface without causing damage. This is especially vital when you start installing more elaborate designs where you are changing patterns within a design. *(See Chapter 14, Pattern Instructions, for photographs of these types of advanced patterns.)*

Chapter 8

EQUIPMENT—TOOLS OF THE ARTIST

Reel and rotary mowers are the two most commonly used mowers. Either mower can produce acceptable results provided they are well maintained and proper mowing practices are followed. For a comparison of the two types, see *Table 1*.

Table 1. Comparison of Rotary and Reel Mower Characteristics

Consideration	Rotary Mower	Reel Mower
Method of cutting	impact; speed of blade	scissors or shearing
Turfgrass	rotation and blade sharpness important	action; blade and bedknife sharpness important
Cutting quality	better for heights above 1 inch; leaf tip fraying common when mower blade moves, bogs down, or blades are not sharp; long grasses and weeds sucked up for cutting	excellent quality for short-cut turf when blades are sharp; may cause longer turf to lay over and not cut cleanly
Maintenance	blades can be easily sharpened by filing or grinding	usually requires professional adjustment and sharpening
Safety	more dangerous; blades revolve at high speed; debris can be thrown	safer; blades revolve more slowly; debris rarely thrown long distances

Consideration	Rotary Mower	Reel Mower
Power requirements	more power required	less power required
Cost	powered models usually less expensive	powered models can be very expensive

Remember, the roller is the key to making stripes when creating a turf pattern. The roller should be the full width of the cutting units and it should be positioned behind the blades of the deck or reel. Some machines, especially reel mowers, will have two rollers—one in front of the reel blades and one behind. This feature helps provide a cleaner cut and more definition in striping. Walk-behind reel mowers can produce vivid contrasts between stripes, since they travel on a larger roller in the back instead of wheels. This larger roller produces additional downward pressure and weight on the grass blades bending in the lines.

Pre-1830 Englishmen with turf lawns used scythes or shears to trim grass. It was very hard work and the results were varied. Englishman Edwin Budding invented the lawnmower in 1830 after watching a cutter in a cloth factory remove the nap from the material. His invention was a reel mower made of cast iron with a front cutting cylinder (reel) that traveled on a big rear roller instead of wheels. It was heavy and hard to maneuver. Horses or people had to supply the power. With the invention of the lawnmower, having a lawn became a status symbol. During the Victorian period people loved the stripes that mowing with machines traveling on rollers left on their lawns as they cut.

Around 1890 gasoline engines and small steam-powered mowers were introduced. Gasoline mowers became popular in 1902. After World War I the lawnmower industry experienced substantial growth. Since then, mowers have become smaller and lighter in weight. Technology has produced mowers that are more cost-efficient than ever before. Robotic mowers are now beginning to show up on the market. The day may come when we can relax in air-conditioned comfort as a preprogrammed unit applies a pattern. Pictured are some old and new mowers that can be used to produce patterns.

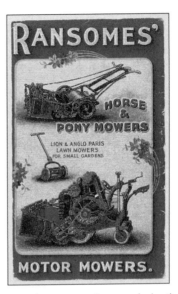

First lawnmower, made in 1830 by Edwin Budding, featuring a large roller that created a pattern known as the "banded finish" throughout England. Photo courtesy of The British Lawn Mower Museum.

Horse and pony power. Ransomes' advertisement shows the true meaning of horsepower. Photo courtesy of The British Lawn Mower Museum.

1860 horse-drawn mower including the leather boots worn by the horse to prevent damage to the turf from the horses' hooves. Photo courtesy of The British Lawn Mower Museum.

1890 horse-drawn gang mower. One man guided the mower, while another walked the horse checking the turf for stones and other debris that could cause mower damage. Photo courtesy of The British Lawn Mower Museum.

In Victorian times the lawn patterns created by early mowers was a status symbol as evidenced in this advertisement featuring an English castle. Advertisements courtesy of The British Lawn Mower Museum.

This mower was pulled by manpower. It was designed to mow between gravestones in the late nineteenth century. Photo courtesy of The British Lawn Mower Museum.

1955 Qualcast Panther lawn mower owned by English actress Jean Alexander, known from Coronation Street as "Hilda Ogden." Photo courtesy of The British Lawn Mower Museum.

My father with a push reel mower, commonly used during the 1940s. Photo courtesy of Marjorie Mellor.

Toro's 3500 Grounds Master Side Winder. This tri-plex mower features reels that can be shifted side to side. This design feature was intended to make mowing around golf course bunkers safer, but can also be utilized in creating unique mowing patterns. Photo courtesy of The Toro Company.

This John Deere 2653 triplex mower, commonly used on golf course fairways, is perfect for use on sports fields, and a great pattern maker. Photo courtesy of The John Deere Company.

A John Deere 21-inch walk-behind reel mower. This single reel unit is good for mowing baseball infields, and other small areas, such as the penalty area on a soccer field. Photo courtesy of The John Deere Company.

Nonmotorized reel mower, by Thomas Green and Sons, Leeds, England. A person or horse supplied the power. The bar in front can be used with a towrope. This mower was often used on private tennis courts in the early twentieth century. Milton Keynes Museum. Photo courtesy of Keith Wootton, Old Lawn Mower Club, England.

A 1920 motorized version of the popular Messor Silens, Latin for silent mower. Milton Keynes Museum. Photo courtesy of Keith Wootton, Old Lawn Mower Club, England.

A 1930 Dennis mower. Company based in Guildford, England. The roller under the seat helped define the pattern. Photo courtesy of Keith Wootton, Old Lawn Mower Club, England.

The full-width roller mounted on the back of this Simplicity rotary deck enables operators to make patterns as they mow. Photo Courtesy of Simplicity Manufacturing.

Lawn tractors, like the Simplicity Regent, often have rollers that help in applying a decorative pattern to your lawn. Photo Courtesy of Simplicity Manufacturing.

This Derby zero-turn mower, the "Stallion," makes a nice choice for landscapers and homeowners. Photo Courtesy of Simplicity Manufacturing.

To make bold patterns on large lawns, sports fields and other managed landscapes, look for features like the Free Floating™ deck, and full-width rollers on tractors like this Simplicity Legacy. Photo Courtesy of Simplicity Manufacturing.

This Massey Ferguson is equipped with a Free Floating™ mowing deck and rollers manufactured by Simplicity. It's a good pattern-maker. Photo Courtesy of Simplicity Manufacturing.

This Simplicity lawn tractor features a zero-turning radius which is nice for confined spaces. It makes mowing around trees and other obstacles easy, while rollers mounted on the mowing deck help you apply a nice pattern. Photo Courtesy of Simplicity Manufacturing.

Mower Care

After each use, shut down the mower's engine and allow it to cool. Disconnect the spark plug and clean the blades or reels and under the mower deck. Don't wash a hot mower, as water splashed onto the engine or cutting units could crack the engine block or warp the cutting blades. For good vacuum—which aides in a clean cut and a good discharge of clippings—remove debris that tends to collect under decks and reels to ensure good air circulation under the deck. Water from a hose will help, but you might need to physically scrape the clippings out. Be sure to disconnect the spark plug *before* scraping under the deck or around blades.

To prevent damp grass from clogging the discharge shoot of a rotary mower deck, Milwaukee TV handyman Gus Gnorsky shared this tip: Pressure-wash the underside of the deck, cleaning it thoroughly. Rub the discharge shoot with steel wool to ensure a better paint bond, then wipe with a mild acetone solvent to be sure it's clean. Paint the discharge shield and 6 inches into the exit shoot with a urethane oil-based, high-gloss paint. Allow to cure for approximately 72 hours. This will provide a hard, slick surface that wet grass will not stick to and clump, while aiding the overall maintenance by preventing rust and making the deck easier to clean.

The key to a quality cut with any style of mower is to be certain it has sharp, well-adjusted blades. Dull, poorly adjusted blades tear rather than cut the grass, leaving it susceptible to disease and giving the lawn a frayed, brownish look. Purchase an extra mower blade for your machine so you can always keep a sharp blade on hand. After removing the dull blade, have it sharpened at an equipment repair service so you'll be ready when the new blade dulls. The frequency of changing the blade is limited only by your ambitions. Many professional turf managers change blades or adjust them daily. Changing it once a month would be a good start. For best results, mow when the turf is dry to prevent clumping.

Rollers

If you want to start making patterns, but don't have a reel mower or a rotary mower with rollers attached, don't worry. You can still make a lovely pattern; it will just take a little more time and effort. You can buy or rent a lawn roller that you can use to bend in patterns. A roller

This is a photo of an add-on roller kit, which is attached to an Ariens walk-behind rotary mower. This type of roller kit turns a regular rotary mower into a pattern-making machine.

Photo courtesy of Ariens Company.

is a hollow drum with a drain plug, which can be removed so the drum can be filled with water to add weight. Adjust the weight so that the roller is not too heavy to comfortably push. The extra weight will add pressure to bend in your pattern. It is important that the roller not be too heavy, as it could cause deep compaction of the root zone, harming the health of the grass. *(See photo page 83.)*

Using a Roller

Plan your mowing direction so that the tire marks from the mower will not distract from the pattern you install. After mowing the turf area with your rotary mower you can start rolling in your pattern. Follow the same principles and steps described in Chapter 14, Pattern Instructions. To get more detail in your pattern you may have to repeat each stripe, or every other stripe, depending on the weight of the roller and the grass surface you are patterning.

Landscape contractors use this method quite successfully. Even without a mower that makes patterns, many use rollers to provide a beautiful patterned finish on a client's yard.

Making a Roller

If you cannot or do not want to rent or purchase a large roller, you can make a smaller one.

You will need:
a rotary push mower handle bar
two 3- to 4-inch-long threaded carriage bolts (to fit through
    the holes in at the base of the handlebar)
washers and nuts to fit
cement mix or QuickCrete®
A section of PVC pipe, 3-6 inches in diameter, 24-36 inches long
wood circles cut to fit inside pipe or duct tape
a tape measure

Step 1. Lawnmower repair shops usually have salvage push rotary mowers, in what is often known as the "graveyard." Speak to the manager and explain that you need an old, used mower handle to recycle into a "pattern tool." Make it clear that you would like to have one—or purchase one for a nominal fee—from a mower in the graveyard. Most stores are happy to oblige. Some may ask you to remove the handle yourself, so be prepared with a screwdriver, pliers, and wire cutters just in case. Choose a long handle, especially if you are tall.

Step 2. Once you have obtained the mower handle, determine the width of stripe you want to make. Somewhere between 20 and 36 inches is a good size. Remember, the wider the roller, the heavier it will be and the harder it will be to push. If you choose a width that is greater than the width of your handle, you can gently bend the handle ends to fit the pipe. Choose a 3- or 6-inch-diameter PVC pipe, keeping in mind that the larger the diameter the heavier it will be when filled with cement.

Step 3. Purchase two threaded 3- or 4-inch-long carriage bolts fitted with nuts and washers sized to fit the existing hole in the mower handle.

Step 4. There are two ways to securely close the PVC pipe: The first is to tape one end of the PVC pipe securely closed with the duct tape. The second is to drill a pilot hole in the center of the wood circles and

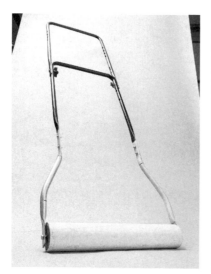

This homemade roller features extended handles made from electrical conduit. This makes it easier to push for taller people. Photo courtesy of Peter Henandez.

A roller used on an English bowling lawn. Photo courtesy of Mike Beard, The Groundsman, England.

place the bolts through them, then fit one circle into the pipe with the bolt's threaded end facing out.

Step 5. Mix the cement as directed on the package. When thoroughly mixed, slowly fill the PVC pipe. After the pipe is filled and the cement has settled, tape the remaining end closed or fit it with the wood insert, again with the bolt's threaded end exposed.

Step 6. (If not using wood inserts) Find the exact center of the pipe diameter on each end. Poke a guide hole in the duct tape, then sink in a bolt, headfirst, approximately 2 inches, leaving 1 inch of the threads exposed. Be careful to keep the bolt perpendicular. Let the cement set to harden for the recommended length of time.

Step 7. After the cement is thoroughly cured, attach the handle to the PVC roller. Slip the bolts through the holes in the handlebar, add washers, and tighten the nuts onto the bolts.

You are now ready to use your new tool. Follow the pattern instruction included in this book or design your own.

Other Equipment for Striping

While a roller makes a beautiful striped pattern, there are also other tools you can utilize to make or remove a pattern. Some examples are a drag mat, lawn sweeper, hand roller, squeegee, or golf green roller. The Toro HydroJect® and the VertiDrain® aerators have rollers that assist in aerating. These rollers produce a stripe as they travel. When we use these at the stadium, we plan ahead of time which direction we want them to go according to the stripes they make. We carefully decide which directions to have the aerators travel so the stripe does not interfere with the existing pattern or one we will be installing. We emphasize straight lines that are consistent in width, just like with a mower. At times, the lines created by the aerator actually compliment the mower line patterns.

This roller can also be used to create designs. Photo Courtesy of the Gandy Company.

Chapter 9
PREVENTING TRAFFIC AND WEAR PROBLEMS

Practicing the basics of turfgrass management will help encourage healthy, actively growing grass plants. These practices include aerating the soil to relieve compaction of the growing medium. Have a soil test done to determine the soil's nutrient levels and follow the suggested fertilization program. At the stadium we use recommendations from soil testing as our guide, then apply extra potassium (K_2O) in our fertilization program to increase our plants' tolerance to stress, disease, and wear. We also apply calcium (Ca) to boost our plants' ability to deal with stress. Liquid applications of calcium can be used during the heat of summer or after an event when the grass is limp and lying down to invigorate and help it stand back up.

Consider these tips to prevent traffic and wear problems. As mentioned earlier, it's important agronomically to rotate the directions of your stripes. You will enhance the overall health of your turfgrass plants by changing your patterns and you will prevent excess wear caused by repetitive lines. By changing the design you will also benefit from the practice and from the challenge of making new designs. This practice will help you earn your stripes.

Pattern Rotation
Compaction to the root zone (sand, native soil, or blend) when mowing the same design can create a wear pattern. Mowing the same pattern over weeks or repetitively on wet ground can cause tire marks and ruts and affect surface levelness. When this happens you can scalp the turfgrass plants with the mowing blades. Not only is this injury to the plants aesthetically unpleasant, it could also kill the turfgrass due to problems associated with the compaction and ruts.

Turn Carefully

Be careful when making your turns on the mower. Do not turn corners quickly. Slow down before and during turns to prevent the
mower tires from damaging the grass. Refer to Chapter 7, Making
Turns With Your Mower, to learn techniques on how to make careful
turns and prevent damage.

Overseed

It's easier to prevent a problem than to deal with the results of poor
management afterward. Small yet frequent amounts of overseeding
with your desired turfgrass species and cultivars can provide a big
benefit. It's important not to apply a heavy amount of seed at one
time. It's better to seed more often at a lower rate. Be proactive if you
know in advance that a pattern may have wear or stress areas. Start
lightly overseeding those spots even before you install the pattern for
the first time. Then overseed as you see wear areas start to develop.
Depending on the species of grass or grasses used, if in two weeks you
see additional wear in those locations, lightly overseed again.
Continue this process as needed. It will result in plant growth in different stages and hopefully prevent the area from getting too worn.

Use a topdressing similar to your soil mix to help with establishment and prevent multiple layering of different soil types, as this
could cause drainage problems. Before spreading, you can mix the
seed with a product such as Penn Mulch® or Seed Aide® to help with
germination. Follow product label directions for accurate application.

Wetness

It's best to mow in dry conditions, but there are times when you have
to mow even though the root zone is damp. The mower tires can
track the soil mix onto the grass blades, leaving discolored stains.
These stains are very conspicuous on a pattern. Inspect the grass area
by walking over it first to locate wet spots. When making the pattern,
avoid that area by working around it or eliminate entirely the lines
that will encompass that area.

Another way to manage a problem wet spot is to speed up the drying process by topdressing it with calcined clay (similar to the
material that nonclumping kitty litter is made of). This will serve two

functions: It will help dry up the excess moisture and provide a small interface between the wet root zone and the tires on your mower.

If the root zone is very wet, holes can be punched into the ground and then backfilled with calcined clay. This will place more product into the root zone, which provides instant drying, and in the future it will prevent the area from becoming too wet. Calcined clay can also be used after core aerating. Topdress with calcined clay over the grass surface and broom or drag it into the aeration holes. Profile Products' Turface® soil conditioner is a calcined clay product available from lawn product suppliers.

Crum Rubber®

Dr. John Rogers III and his staff at Michigan State University have researched, developed, and patented a new product called Crum Rubber® to combat turf wear. All royalties paid to Michigan State are dedicated to turfgrass research. A product example of this is Crown III®, which is made of recycled tires. It's black and thus absorbs heat, and can be mixed with seed and topdressing mix. This very interesting product is manufactured by recycling the rubber from tires into small crumb-sized particles that can be topdressed over the turf. The rubber particles act as a cushion or shock absorber for the crown of the turfgrass plant. The use of Crown III® does not reduce the need for good turf management practices, but it does provide extra wear tolerance. It's easy to use and is a nice tool to have in those areas that experience extra wear from specific patterns. When you change patterns the plants in the treated areas will continue to benefit from the Crum Rubber®. Follow recommended application rates for best results.

Mowers

The Toro Company recently introduced a new mower called the SideWinder®. It has cutting units that can be shifted side to side, thus enabling you to offset your tire marks. This feature is useful in preventing repeat wear from following the same tire marks.

If the turfgrass surface that you're mowing isn't level (and most are not), it's important that your cutting blades be able to undulate with the contours of the surface. Most reel mowers in proper working condition will do this. Check your specific model for this feature and be sure it is in working order.

Rotary mowers are a different story. If the mowing deck doesn't follow the contours of the mowing surface, they can easily scalp the turfgrass plants and create even more problems by digging into your soil. Unfortunately, I found this out the hard way. I saw the disastrous results of a big commercial rotary mower at the ballpark when it didn't "float" and some turf was damaged. At my home I have used a Simplicity Landlord garden tractor which has a patented Free Floating™ deck with full-width rollers. I've been very pleased with these features. The Free Floating™ deck follows the contour changes in the ground, so it gives a clean cut without scalping the turf. Also, the full-width rollers allow me the ability to create patterns just like at a stadium. *(See Chapter 8, Equipment—Tools of the Artist, for more details.)*

Chapter 10

TECHNIQUES TO HELP HIDE DAMAGED TURF

Expectations are on the rise throughout the turf industry when it comes to aesthetics. Homeowners and businesses want their lawns to look like the professional fields and golf courses they visit and see on television. Park administrators, professional sports team owners, and management want the best turf surface available. A nicely groomed turf with a striped pattern provides the perfect backdrop for an event and serves to distinguish a complex or sports field. These demands add pressure on the turf care manager to produce a safe, playable field and to enhance its aesthetics. A healthy turf can withstand a great deal of use, but it does have limits. Even under the best turf management program wear and tear can take its toll on grass plants. Professional athletic fields, collegiate fields, park districts, and home lawns will all show the stresses associated with inclement weather, wear, and, if improperly installed, patterns. Masking the resulting turf damage can improve the overall appearance of the grass.

A safe field is a must. Safety and playability of an athletic field should be the first priority of any sports turf manager, whether professional leagues or children's leagues. Any damage that presents safety concerns must be fixed promptly and correctly. Don't try to hide hazardous damage. Athletes shouldn't have to worry about the playing surface; it's the responsibility of the field supervisor that the field play true. Once safety and playability issues are addressed, then you can beautify the surface by striping the turf with a pattern.

The choice of a mowing pattern is important. When choosing a pattern for sports fields, be certain the design does not affect the play of the game. The pattern should enhance the beauty of the field while not being distracting, and allow the players to concentrate on the game.

Even the best fields suffer wear damage, and how it is managed is crucial to the turf's appearance. Different sports cause different concentrations of wear on athletic fields. Normal wear on baseball fields is frequently seen around home plate, the on-deck areas, in front of the pitcher's mound, and by the coaches' boxes at first and third bases. On a football field it's common for the grass in the center of the field and between the hash marks to become worn. Soccer fields exhibit the first signs of wear near the goal areas.

If you mow the same pattern too often the tire marks create extra wear and the locations where you make turns will show visible signs of repetitive action. While these high-traffic wear areas may not present a safety issue, they do have a negative impact on the aesthetics of the grass surface. Even areas in the home yards where children play repetitively will show damage. Due to budgets, weather, and/or time constraints, resodding or reseeding aren't always viable options.

Following are some quick fixes—basic practices you can use to help hide cosmetic damage that can affect the aesthetics of your turf.

Mowing Patterns

Mowing patterns can be utilized to hide or mask worn areas. A pleasing pattern can dress up a thin, worn turf, or draw the eye away from damaged areas and focus it on a patterned spot. Masking damage with a pattern works best when the stripes are made of narrow widths and have repetitive lines. This type of pattern will change the direction of the bend in the turf blades, providing more light and dark stripes to conceal the damaged area.

Green Colorants

Many athletic field managers, golf course superintendents, and even some homeowners have used green dye to paint the turf at one time or another. Colorant will make the discolored turf more aesthetically appealing, and it can help the grass. The darkened shade of green applied will absorb more light and heat and can help generate new growth and healing. During the summer drought of 1999 I heard news reports of paint companies marketing green latex paint to homeowners in the eastern United States for touching up lawns that had suffered the effects of the extreme weather.

Colorants come premixed, as a powder or concentrated liquid to be mixed with water. Finding a colorant that produces a natural grass

When viewing this photo you tend to concentrate on the vivid pattern. Your attention is drawn toward the intriguing details and you find yourself wondering how it was made before you see the worn areas. You overlook the worn area around home plate, or at least it's not as apparent. Photos courtesy of Tom Nielson.

green color versus a bluish green can be difficult. I have tested quite a few throughout my career in turfgrass management. Becker Underwood makes a liquid product call Green Lawnger® that is easy to mix and use, but most importantly it provides a beautiful shade of green. Most colorants are applied with a boom sprayer for large areas and sprayed with a handheld or backpack pump sprayer for smaller areas. The colorant could be brushed on, but the process is tedious and the results not as good.

If you use dye or latex paint (not oil-based paint—it will kill the grass!) be sure to follow all mixing directions. Experience has taught me to begin mixing the concentration at an even lower rate than the label states. I have also found that to find the rate that works best it's good to practice on a test area out of view of the spectators. Test on an area of similar condition and discoloration to the primary site you're treating. Carefully blend the color-treated grass where it meets the healthier grass. Paint small areas at a time. Begin painting with lighter shades of green color. It is easier to add more coats of paint to make it darker than to try to remove the green paint once it gets too dark. Walk away from the treated area often to see how it looks from a distance. View it from several angles, including from the spectator stands. It's easy for the paint to become too dark quickly. What looks fine up close while you are applying the dye can stick out from afar by being too dark. Your goal is to make the entire area uniform by matching the healthy grass. You don't want it to look like you painted it.

Topdressing Sand
When you are seeding in thin areas or for repairing divots, topdressing sand can be painted green and mixed with grass seed. You can purchase it prepainted or paint it yourself. The green sand will hide the damage until the new seed gets established. I have successfully used this method to fill divots and topdress over thin areas on athletic fields.

Grass Clippings
Fresh grass clippings saved from mowing can be spread over worn or damaged spots. This is an inexpensive and very effective way to hide damaged, thin areas for the day or for an event. From a distance it will blend in with the surrounding healthy grass and be barely noticeable.

In this photo grass clippings were used by the on-deck circles to hide bare topsoil. Photo by David R. Mellor.

Looking at this photo you notice the dazzling pattern. What you do not immediately notice are the areas that were bare topsoil until I point them out. The lighter areas at the edge of the track by the on-deck circles are where worn grass was removed with a sod cutter. The sod was removed on Friday and the area was prepared for new sod to be laid on Monday.

As I describe in Chapter 14 in the instructions for "The Wave," I received a phone call from Diller and Scofidio on Friday night asking for a virtually matchless design. My daughter drew this one for me with crayons. I wanted to install and photograph the pattern as soon as possible, but I realized the prepared sod site would show in the photo and not be acceptable for the art exhibit project. I didn't have the sod available to install so I improvised. I put the grass-catching baskets on the triplex reel mower and caught enough clippings to hide these two very visible spots. No other techniques were needed to camouflage the dark black topsoil, which was so noticeable before the clippings were spread. This procedure works best when the clippings are used the same day. They will spread more easily if they are dry. Do not apply the clippings deeper than ¼ to ½ inch thick or they could affect the play on the athletic field or harm the remaining live grass. Keep the saved clippings stored in the shade to retain the color and cover them with a cool, moist towel to help hold in the moisture. A friend and colleague, Steve Wightman, Turf Manager at Qualcomm Stadium in San Diego, has suggested storing the clippings on ice on a hot summer day to keep them cool and to hold a fresh-cut look.

At the end of the day you must remove the used clippings. If left on the turf the clippings will discolor and produce a rancid smell. They can even cause additional damage to your grass. Remember, this is a temporary solution.

Conclusion

Used appropriately, each of the techniques mentioned can mask damaged areas for the big game or home party. Used alone or together, these methods will help you present your best-looking grass. Any condition that presents a safety concern, especially on athletic fields, should be dealt with promptly. Take the necessary steps to bring the turf back to a safe condition. Don't try to hide or mask an area that could cause physical injury. Correct It!

Take pictures and make notes of damaged areas for future reference. When time and budget allow, sod to bring the turf back to standard. Areas that show repeated damage may need to be managed with more care and attention. Utilize good cultural practices of aeration, irrigation, and proper mowing height and frequency. Consider having a soil test performed on those locations to fine tune the fertilization program implemented there.

Chapter 11

USEFUL TIPS

Managing Sun Glare

Many athletic field and golf course managers mow early in the morning. It can be difficult to see the pattern line, even in an established pattern, when mowing into the bright rising sun. Often, because of field use requirements, the mowing cannot be delayed and must be done promptly. When the sun is not high enough to accentuate the lines there are several approaches to take:

1. Wear a baseball cap, cowboy hat, or other headgear with a long or wide brim to shade your eyes from the sun.

2. Wear quality sunglasses to cut down glare.

3. If you're wearing both hat and sunglasses and you are still having difficulty seeing, try lightly watering the grass. A fine mist of water on the surface of the grass will bring out the light and dark stripes. It's important that you use a very small amount of water, and barely wet the grass blades. The water droplets will make the grass blades just wet enough to help you better see the pattern, yet not so wet that it interferes with the quality of the cut, causes clippings to build up and clog the blades, causes compaction of the soil, or makes the grass surface slippery or unsafe. Alone or combined with the other two recommendations, this procedure will be a significant help in completing your pattern.

Keeping it Straight

When using a walk-behind reel mower be careful to line up correctly at the beginning of each line. If you have to stop the mower at the end of one line before starting the next, it's easy to start out crooked.

Since one hand is on the handlebar and the other hand is used to engage the traction traveling gear, the mower may pull toward the side of the handlebar your hand is on. Place the hand that's on the handlebar in the middle before the mower is put into gear. With the guide hand in the middle, the mower is less likely to shift to the side. Also, to lessen shifting, engage the mower at a slower RPM when starting the stripe. Once it is straight, after walking a step or two you can increase the RPMs.

Rolling Along

Many athletic fields, golf courses, and home lawns have surface undulations or crowns, which can pose challenges when you are trying to create long straight lines. The mower tends to follow the contour of the ground and shift slightly to one side or the other. It's helpful to pick a focal point in the distance that is aligned with the stripe you are mowing. Should a bend in the line develop, go back two lines and reset the straight edge.

The End of the Line

When mower operators have to stop in mid-stripe it can mar the straightness of the line. For the health of the grass, and for operator safety, all blades should be stopped. When operators are ready to start mowing again, they should lift the reels or deck, back up 2 to 3 feet, then put the reels or deck down, start moving forward, and turn on the blades simultaneously. By starting 2 to 3 feet behind where they stopped, operators will be able to be on line. Milwaukee Brewers ground crew members wait at the end of the line that is being mowed or rolled, and talk there, not at mid-stripe, unless it's an emergency. This common courtesy may seem minor, but it is helpful to mower operators, enabling them to complete the pattern more accurately.

Watch Your Step

The movements of athletes, golfers, children, and golf carts cannot always be controlled when it comes to where or how they walk or travel on a patterned grass. However, employees, greens crews, ground crews, and maintenance crews can follow some simple steps to prevent unnecessary footprints and wheel marks against the grain of a pattern. In Milwaukee we stress to ground crew members that they be aware of how they walk onto and off the field, especially during pregame preparation work. They need to remember to lift their feet so they're not scuffing or dragging their feet through the grass, which may disrupt the pattern. When possible, we prefer they walk on the light-colored stripes. (Remember: Light stripes are made by traveling away from the vantage point; dark stripes are made by traveling toward the vantage point.)

Traffic Patterns

Be careful driving equipment on and off patterned grass, as stray tire marks over a pattern will detract from its beauty. When it's necessary to move a wheelbarrow or other vehicle across the grass, enter and exit on a light-colored stripe when possible. When equipment must be taken to the infield of a baseball field, I recommend taking it on and off near the umpire's spot behind first or third base. This is usually a shorter distance to travel over grass, and results in shorter tire tracks. The first and third base locations are also off to the side of the main viewing angle. The grass space from behind home plate to the warning track is small in size, but tire marks will be more obvious because of its prime location.

These steps and techniques will become second nature with a little practice. By following these suggestions, you'll be able to offset the "out of control" factors associated with creating a pattern.

Color-Coded Maintenance

On days when your time is limited or the grass is under stress from weather or events, it's best not to mow your entire turfgrass surface. On these days, use "color-coded maintenance" (i.e., the "every other line" procedure: mow either all of the light stripes or all of the dark stripes in the design) as a tool to incorporate your pattern. Once your chosen pattern is established you'll avoid having to mow the entire grass area by implementing the "every other line" technique as a tool to perk up your pattern.

Start by retracing every other line with the roller, transporting it around until you complete all the light or dark stripes on that angle. Then do the same "every other line" procedure on the other angle. This method will freshen up your pattern using only half the time it would take to mow all the grass. You can also use this technique to prevent losing a pattern over time. Use the original lines as a guide and trace over every other line, etching in the design. While some of you may mow every day, many others do not have the time or the workforce for it. I recommend you do color-coded maintenance between mowings to keep a crisp, detailed pattern when you cannot mow it all but still want a professional look.

Chapter 12
HOW PATTERNS ARE CREATED

I've been asked countless times—in person, through phone calls, and in letters—how stripes are made on grass. Articles on patterning have appeared in periodicals as diverse as the *Cleveland Plain Dealer*, *Popular Mechanics*, *Men's Health*, and *House and Garden*. A wide range of myths exist on how patterns are created, ranging from being painted in varying shades of green to alternating types of grasses, mowing at different heights, and being fertilized differently. It's not as mysterious as you might think. A pattern is created when the grass blades are bent in the direction the mower is traveling by a roller mounted behind the cutting blades. The roller provides downward pressure to bend the grass blades so that reflecting light forms alternate dark and light stripes.

When you're mowing and you get to the end of the line you're making and you turn around, the light stripe you just made will now appear dark. *Stripes or shapes that look light when viewed from one direction will look dark from the other direction, and vice versa.* Remembering this will keep you from getting confused when developing your designs.

While any mower will make a pattern of some type, those lines are usually made by tire marks or the spinning action of the cutting reels or rotary blades. Landscape commercial front deck mowers like Stiener, Stag, and Ransome can produce patterns. Any stripes created in this manner don't last long and fail to have the polished look of a pattern made by rollers. In order to create a lasting pattern design you need a roller behind the cutting blades to bend the turfgrass. Most reel mowers have some type of roller mounted behind the cutting blades. It is important that these rollers are sized to fit the full width of the mower blades. A solid, smooth roller will perform much better than a grooved or slotted roller.

To date most rotary mowers don't have rollers as part of the equipment. Simplicity Manufacturing of Port Washington, Wisconsin is the only company who manufactures a full line of lawn and garden tractors and riding mowers available with the full-width rollers necessary to stripe your lawn. However, this is beginning to change. Other manufacturers have become aware of mowing patterns and are now offering a roller as part of their machine, a bonus feature devoted to aesthetics. They realize that mowing patterns have become a signature of quality with sports turfgrass managers, home lawn enthusiasts, and corporate green space and landscape contractors. Greater details on equipment options, including photographs of rotary mowers with rollers, are provided in Chapter 8, Equipment—Tools of the Artist.

Begin by mowing the first pass in one direction, then transport back around to where you started. After offsetting your position, mow the next uncut area adjacent to the one just mowed. By mowing in only one direction you will be bending all the grass blades in the same direction, making it totally one color. That way you won't be competing with the mower lines when using your smaller walk-behind mower to create a pattern.

At times I will mow the infield from first base to third base—or horizontal to where the pattern will be viewed from most—in alternating directions, actually making stripes that are visible from the sides yet do not show up when viewed from behind home plate. These lines and tire marks are not as noticeable, whether cut with a reel or rotary mower. During the 1991-1993 major league baseball seasons, the Milwaukee Brewers club management requested that the infield grass be cut at a height of 2¼ to 3 inches. The rationale was that the extra height of the grass might slow the ball enough to enable our fleet infielders (Robin Vount, Paul Molitor, Jim Gantner, Pat Listach, and Billy Spiers) to reach the ball and make a play.

We accomplished this height by mowing with a walk-behind rotary mower instead of our reel mower. We mowed from first to third base so the tire marks wouldn't interfere with the patterns, which were then created with a walk-behind reel mower (the reel mower's blades were turned off and only the rollers were in use to apply the designs). I learned through trial and error. The old saying "Practice, Practice, Practice" is painfully true. Practice continues to help me and I am sure it will help you too.

I'm often asked, "How do you make your checkerboard, diamond, and crossing patterns jump out so vividly?" The answer is quite simple. Once you have mowed both angles for your design, you're ready to bring out the depth of the pattern. When you mow both angles the same day, the last set of stripes you mow will be the more dominant. The last mowing direction you traveled goes over the top of the first set of lines you made, causing the first set of lines to be smudged by the second set. Once both angles are applied to your turfgrass, go back and mow or roll every other line of the first angle. Choose the light or dark lines and with the rollers down—but the cutting blades off—skip every other line and then travel around your pattern. This traveling pass can be done on the grass and then incorporated into the design as part of a cleanup pass, or it can be done on the warning track or the edge of the baselines. This procedure goes more quickly than mowing because most mowers can travel faster in the transporting gear than with the cutting blades engaged. You can also travel more quickly because you don't have to worry about the cutting blades giving a clean cut at a high ground speed. The little extra time it takes to properly perform this task is time well spent. You will a see a drastic difference when you take the time to use this technique. You don't have to do this each time you mow. Use the technique regularly or save it for a special game or tournament. When I want to add depth drama to a pattern I'll do this to fine-tune and separate the lines and bring out the bold contrast within the design.

When a pattern is being made it's the rollers that bend the grass blades, thereby creating the design. These rollers etch in the stripe, light or dark, in the direction you are traveling. A roller on a reel mower or rotary mower can be used while the reels are engaged and cutting or when the reels or rotary blades are disengaged but with the rollers down on the turf. Use only the rollers to create a new pattern, enhance a pattern, or just freshen up the sections of existing designs. I use the rollers in each of these ways.

On a baseball field the main viewing angle is from behind home plate looking toward the outfield. The high home camera shot emphasizes the field best for television. When the mower travels in the direction from first base to third base or across the field, the pattern doesn't show up dramatically from behind home plate. Consider this before making those lines and thinking they will show vividly in your design. Because this mowing direction across the field is not as noticeable, it can serve an important role. When mowing a pattern over several weeks to make it brilliant, a grain could develop. To clean up grass lines within that design, and redirect the grain but not affect the aesthetics of the design, mow across the field.

This same concept can be used when making more complex designs on the infield or when mowing with a rotary mower that does not have a roller. Mow the crossing direction, then come back using a roller to install the true design.

Our Kentucky bluegrass/perennial ryegrass blend is currently cut in the range of 1⅛ and 1¼ inches high. I'll first cut one or two cleanup passes with a basket catching clippings on the reel nearest the edge so I don't have to mow over the edge. This prevents throwing clippings onto the baselines, warning track, or infield skin area. To ensure a clean cut on our infield, I mow it all in one direction the first day, and then change to the opposite direction the next. By this I mean that I mow from first to third base, then transport around and mow from first to third again. I repeat this action until all the infield or grass area has been cut. The next mowing, I reverse the direction by mowing from third to the first base line. Changing direction prevents the grass from lying down and starting a grain in the turf . When all the grass has been cut, I then use a walk-behind reel mower, with the reels disengaged, using only the rollers on the machine to create the pattern. This procedure, combined with mowing in one direction, will help achieve a more polished finish. This concept can be tailored to your own situation, depending on the size of your turf area and the chosen pattern.

Mowing a turfgrass area this way is especially helpful when creating a more complex pattern with a walk-behind reel mower that you may have to turn around within that area. When you're mowing a pattern with a walk-behind reel mower you must be careful not to leave any uncut grass blades in turn areas. As with any mower, it is important to overlap the previous line just enough to cut all the grass in the current pass, yet not so much that the width of the line is changed. When installing a more intricate pattern it can be even easier to miss some blades of grass. On sports turf, if you mow in the morning and leave some grass uncut between stripes, the thin lines of uncut grass will become more evident by an evening game and not provide the manicured look you're striving for.

This same idea of mowing with a triplex reel mower, then coming back with a walk-behind reel mower and using the rollers to roll in the lines can be a special way to put a decorative pattern on a soccer field in the 18 meter penalty box area and mid circle or on a football field in the end zone or in 5- or 10-yard sections between yard lines. (See color plates 1, 2, 3, 40, and 54.)

Chapter 13

PATTERN BASICS

A beautiful basic pattern can be used as the backbone to create more intricate designs. Once your learn the rudimentary techniques they will serve as a guideline for future works of art. You'll have the power to transform ordinary turf into a wonderland of patterns.

A beginning design should start with a concept or drawing. But keep in mind that what works on paper doesn't always translate to turf. With practice—and trial and error—you'll be able to create more elaborate designs and develop a feel for what works best for your site.

Patterns can set a mood. They can represent power and control, or add humor or whimsy. A key to success is to have fun while making your masterpiece.

Mowing a Straight Line

A straight line is important in many patterns. When starting a design with straight lines, use an edge that is established, such as a sideline, foul line, yard line, sidewalk, or driveway. As long as these preexisting lines are in the location you want, they can serve as an easy and accurate starting point. Should those lines not be available, start by making the longest line in your design first. Follow the same concept a farmer uses when planting crops. Pick a point in the distance and focus on it as you mow toward it. Use a focal point, such as an exact spot in the stands, a tree, window, or building. If all else fails set your own predetermined point with a flag. You should periodically glance down approximately 10 feet in front of you as you travel to ensure that you are overlapping, not leaving uncut stripes, while keeping in line with the point you've chosen in the distance. Try to focus primarily on the selected point in the distance. If you only look down at the turf as you mow you can easily lose your perspective and spacing. Should you happen to miss some blades of grass, go back to the

To assist the operator in mowing straight lines, rods were added to this piece of equipment.
Photo by David R. Mellor

previous line, remow it, then recut the line you missed. This way you'll mow the missed section, and by mowing over the lines again you'll etch in those lines.

A straight line can also be accomplished using a line string as a guide. Set two stakes (one on each end of your longest stripe) and draw a string taut between them. Offset your mower just enough so that you don't have to worry about cutting the string. Once you've made passes with the mower on each side of the string, establishing your light and dark lines, and you feel comfortable with the results, you can lift the string and fine-tune the mowing line.

Another way to set sight lines is by attaching to your mower hood one or two rods, or sticks, that can be folded up or down as needed. The two rods act like a gun sight, enabling you to line up the reference point you've picked in the distance. For the markers to work as sites you must sit directly behind them. Line them up between yourself and the point you are focusing on. When using only one marker, it is especially important to keep yourself in exact alignment.

Another simple but effective tool is a wire attached to a hat. I saw this tool used in an English documentary on how crop circles can be created. A wire approximately 6 inches long was twisted together, and a loop the size of a nickel was formed at the end. This wire was then attached to the side of a baseball cap, or from the end of the bill of a cap over the dominant eye. The person then looked through the loop at a point in the distance to stay in alignment.

With practice you will get a feel for your machine. Learn the concept, and you will soon be able to mow by eye. Until then, these tools can be a worthwhile aide to help you with more extensive designs.

Correcting a Crooked Line

It's easy to make a crooked line. The important thing is to fix it and move on. Don't worry if you made a crooked line; it can be straightened quite easily. Fixing it depends on where in your design the line has become crooked. If it happens on the first line you can frame it in on both sides to recreate and set the line. If your line gets crooked-even a little-partway into your design, you must fix it before you go further. Otherwise, the problem will compound, and what was only a minor mistake will grow to the point that it adversely effects your pattern. Go back two lines before the mistake and-using these straight lines as your guide-remow each to reset the errant line. You can always reset a line string if necessary.

Don't get frustrated. You'll get the hang of it before long. You'll be surprised how easy it is to create stunning, detailed patterns once you develop the skills to make a straight line. Armed with this knowledge, you'll develop the special touch needed to be on your way to adding beauty and style with distinctive stripes on your turf. You can use this expertise to continue making designs, both basic and complex, in the future.

Drawing Designs

To get a feel for how a design might look, draw it out before actually applying it on your turf. This can be done in many different ways. Sometimes drawing on a piece of paper is adequate. At a group of field, copy the handy diagram forms in this book and use them as an overlay and guide for drawing and developing patterns for your field.

These forms will enable you to draw a pattern close to scale. Customize the diagrams by making any adjustments that may be unique to your field.

Create a template on your computer to get a more detailed diagram form. Scan the diagrams provided in this book into your computer. Then use a CAD program, PowerPoint®, or similar art program to plan the design. Lay out the field on the screen, then use lines to draw your design. If the lines are repetitive you can have the computer

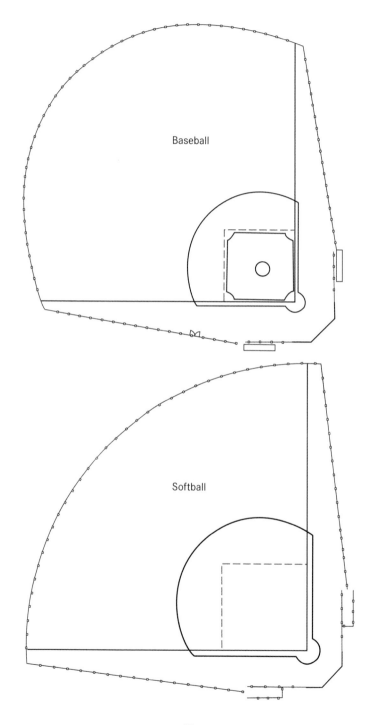

Baseball

Softball

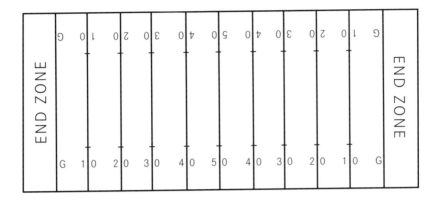

Football

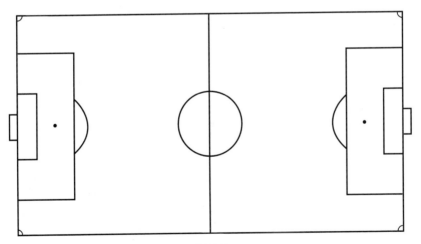

Soccer

Artwork pages 106-108 courtesy James D. Puhalla

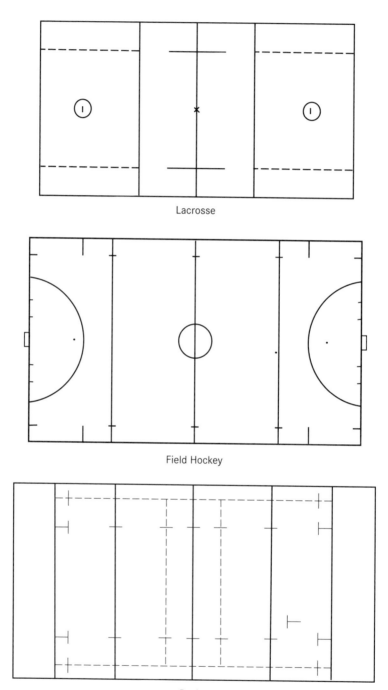

Lacrosse

Field Hockey

Rugby

program repeat the lines until the pattern is completed. You can draw with just lines, then come back and paint in each open section with the appropriate light or dark green color. Remember, the mower traveling away from you on the turfgrass makes a light stripe while the mower traveling toward you makes a dark stripe.

Following are several factors you should consider that can influence how the finished design will look.

Visual Balance

Position the design so that you begin and end with the same color stripe at the beginning and end of a pattern, or within a pattern, to add symmetry to your design.

Proportion

Be sure your pattern's proportion is in scale to your site. For smaller turf areas, long, thin diagonal stripes will add to the perception of a larger space.

Alignment

Determine where your pattern is going to be viewed from most often, then align it so that it is most effective. If there are multiple angles, select an appropriate layout. A diamond pattern or wave works well for a corner yard, taking advantage of an opportunity to use stripes that can be viewed from two angles. Televised Brewers games normally use six to eight camera locations. A Game of the Week production crew may use twenty to twenty-five camera locations. In both situations the pattern we use takes the camera views into consideration.

Site-Specific Factors

Will the pattern be viewed from above or mainly from ground level? If it is viewed primarily from a lower height, keep the main part of the design closer to the viewing area or it might not be seen as well. The details in a more elaborate design will show up better when seen from above. The width of the lines or curves you've chosen has a direct effect on how well they stand out.

The time of day when your pattern will primarily be viewed can make a difference in whether you should feature more light stripes or more dark stripes. Light stripes will show up better at night.

Attention to detail separates a mediocre pattern from a dazzling, manicured display. Your pride will show through your work, making it well worth the time and effort.

Patterns Applied Over Painted Lines

Be careful making pattern stripes perpendicular to painted boundary lines (sidelines, foul lines, yard lines, or hash marks) on athletic fields. A pattern intersecting and crossing a painted line can make it look zigzagged. This is not a concern if the line is going to be repainted. If the line is not going to be repainted, care should be taken before there is a problem. To avoid making a painted line on an athletic field appear crooked, do not drive over it. Don't cross the line—not only with the deck or reels down but even when the blades are up. Stop before the line and make the turn. You can match the stripe on the other side of the line, and the turnaround areas can be erased with a cleanup pass. If a painted line looks crooked it can often be fixed with a broom, leaf rake, or backpack blower, fluffing the edge back up into line.

To make foul lines on a baseball field appear clearer and last longer, consider the perspective of the umpire looking toward the left and right field corners. I recommend mowing the grass outward from the umpire's vantage point. Bending the grass blades in that direction will make the painted white line show up better because there is more grass blade surface for the umpire to see. Mowing in the opposite direction or across the line repeatedly will cause the line to need to be repainted more often.

Erasing a Pattern to Create a New Pattern

Before starting on a new pattern, you may want to lighten or erase the old one. How well an existing pattern can be erased depends on how long it has been established and how much it was ingrained during that time. Sometimes patterns that have been in a short time will be erased as the new stripes are created by the action of the blades and the roller, but designs that have been etched in can take time and encouragement to disappear. This can be accomplished in several ways.

1. **Mow in the opposite direction**—If a pattern is not really bent or burned in the stripes, mowing in the opposite direction—turning

a light stripe dark and a dark stripe light-can erase it. This will bend the grass blades in the opposite direction and stand them more upright.

2. **Use a drag mat**—Stripes can be erased with a drag mat—or a section of cyclone fence—pulled slowly by hand or towed behind a tractor, in the opposite direction of the old stripes. Traveling too fast may fray the ends of the grass blades and damage them. When using this technique it's important to go slow and steady, with careful turns. Trace a light stripe, bending the grass back into a more upright position, turning the strip dark. This will erase the previous line and stand the grass back up. As a result the new pattern will become established sooner, without having to fight old lines that show through the new pattern.

3. **Use a lawn leaf sweeper**—A lawn leaf sweeper pulled against the pattern grain will help erase an old stripe. The spinning brush action of the unit can help remove a pattern, or, used in conjunction with a mower or roller, can help establish a pattern, etching in the design. The only limitation with these units is that they don't turn as easily as mowers, so elaborate designs are more difficult. The small wheels mounted on the base of the sweepers can cut or dig into the turf when a turn is made too quickly or tightly, or if the ground is wet.

4. **Use a broom or leaf rake**—Brooms or leaf rakes work well when erasing the pattern from a small grass area. Gently sweep or rake the stripe in the opposite direction to bend the grass blades upright.

Each of these techniques will help you in going from one pattern to the next. They won't completely erase an existing stripe, but they'll help the new pattern establish sooner.

COLOR PLATES

Plate 1: Denver Broncos' practice facility. Note: Walk behind 1-yard wide lines. This done every other 5-yard section could add an interesting appearance to a football field. Photo courtesy of Troy Smith.

Plate 2: Meadow Lands' checkerboard pattern from goal view. Note the extra detail within the 18-yard box, which adds visual interest. Photo Courtesy of Rob Davis.

Plate 3: Columbus Crew Stadium. Note the different pattern in the goal box of this soccer field. Photo courtesy of Darian Daily.

Plate 4: A nice variation of a plaid design made with both wide and thin lines. Photo courtesy of Kirt Bakos.

Plate 5: I made this pattern after seeing a tartan plaid blanket. The plaid was created with single-wide triplex mower lines, double-wide lines, and groups of walk-behind lines to separate out the design between the big diamonds. Photo by David R. Mellor.

Plate 6: A variation of the plaid pattern. Photo by David R. Mellor.

Plate 7: This pattern varies the width of lines to add depth to the design for Milwaukee County Stadium. Photo by David R. Mellor.

Plate 8: A design inspired by the logo of the Portland Trailblazers. I call it, appropriately, the "Trail Blazer". This is a nice pattern of large grass areas, and is impressive when view from an elevated area, such as an office building. Photo by David R. Mellor.

Plate 9: The "Wave," designed by Cacky Mellor. My daughter created this pattern with her Crayons. Use your imagination when creating new patterns for your lawn, sports field, or golf course. Photo by David R. Mellor.

Plate 10: "Wave" design, opposite view. Photo by David R. Mellor.

Plate 11: A cross view on the Cane County Cougars' field of the "wave" pattern showing the optical illusion of hills that it creates on a flat surface. Photo courtesy of Sarah Martin.

Plate 12: This bull's eye was created on the field of the West Michigan Whitecaps, in Grand Rapids Michigan. This is a nice pattern for soccer fields too. Photo courtesy of Heather Nabozny.

Plate 13: I incorporated the number 19 into this pattern in honor of the Milwaukee Brewers' Robin Yount. Photo by Larry Stoudt.

Plate 14: There are 25 players on a Major League Baseball roster. The #26 was given to Gene Autry, the Angels' team owner. Barney Lopas designed this pattern as a memorial to Mr. Autry. Photo by John Cordes, courtesy of Barney Lopas.

Plate 15: A very crisp "M" incorporated into a design at Milwaukee County Stadium. Photo by David R. Mellor.

Plate 16: Document your patterns to develop a portfolio. It's a good idea to experiment with different film. Pattern picture taken with regular film. Photo by David R. Mellor.

Plate 17: Same pattern as above photographed with infrared film. Using a variety of different film can help show the unique characteristics of your work. Photo Courtesy of Cameron Davidson. © 1997

Plate 18: A big/small checkerboard design at Milwaukee County Stadium. Photo by David R. Mellor.

Plate 19: Traditional checkerboard pattern at one of baseball's great venues, Chicago's Wrigley Field. Photo by Harry Howell, courtesy of All Sport Photography.

Plate 20: A beautiful traditional pattern on bermudagrass at Pro Player Stadium, Miami Florida. Photo courtesy of Alan Sigwardt.

Plate 21: A diagonal cut in the outfield at Milwaukee County Stadium, which produces diamonds in the grass. Photo by David R. Mellor.

Plate 22: Diamond patterns on the infield, and in the outfield. Different mowers were used to create this variety. Photo by David R. Mellor.

Plate 23: This big/small diamond pattern was one I used for 2001 opening day at beautiful Fenway Park in Boston, MA. Photo by David R. Mellor.

Plate 24: Several patterns mowed on to a bermudagrass field. Note how home plate is outlined in the foul play area. Qualcomm Stadium, San Diego, California. Photo courtesy of Steve Wightman.

Plate 25: An abstract pattern I did for The American Lawn: Surfaces of Everyday Life, an internationally touring art exhibit. Photo by David R. Mellor.

Plate 26: This design features overlapping arches that give the grass an allusion of contour. Iowa Cubs' AAA field. Photo courtesy of Luke Yoder.

Plate 27: A pattern I did with the help of a great Brewers ground crew using five wedge sections that I think of as sun rays. The six mowing stripes around the field are cleanup passes to frame in the design. Photo by David R. Mellor.

Plate 28: Here is a pattern at the Iowa Cubs' field that uses the mound as the center point.

Photo Courtesy of Luke Yoder.

Plate 29: Mark Razum and his crew of the Colorado Rockies did this awesome pattern for the 1997 All-Star game. Photo courtesy of Rich Clarkson & Associates.

Plate 30: With the support of a talented grounds grew, this elaborate pattern required only two days for me to complete. The 2000, AAA All Star Game in Rochester, New York. Photo David R. Mellor. Design by Catherine and Victoria Mellor.

Plate 31: The same pattern as above viewed from the outfield. Photo by David R. Mellor.

Plate 32: Here a crew member uses a boom to fine-tune the design for the AAA All Star Game in Rochester, New York. Photo David R. Mellor.

Plate 33: A multi-directional cut on bermudagrass at Dodger Stadium, Los Angeles, California. Mark Razum created this infield pattern in the late 1980's while with the Oakland A's. It does not require lining up stripes through the mound, and by mowing only the sides of the mound it also reduces the wear and tear to the mound area. Photo by Tom Hauck, courtesy of All Sport Photography.

Plate 34: An easy-to-do arching pattern on a baseball infield. Arches are decorative, but do not require the same technical skill necessary to cut a pattern that is divided by the pitcher's mound. Photo by David R. Mellor.

Plate 35: Square within a square pattern in infield. This design creates the illusion of the field being raised. Photo by David R. Mellor.

Plate 36: Interesting infield pattern on zoysiagrass at Bank One Ballpark. Photo courtesy of Sean Mantucca.

Plate 37: This pattern at Bank One Ballpark in Phoenix, Arizona, is mowed on zoysiagrass. Photo courtesy of Sean Mantucca.

Plate 38: A combination of patterns at the home of the West Michigan Whitecaps, and Grand Rapids, Michigan. Photo courtesy of Heather Nabozny.

Plate 39: Warm-season grasses that are over seeded with perennial rye grass produce nice patterns too. Photo courtesy of the University of Houston Athletic Department

Plate 40: 1993 Super Bowl field showing traditional 5-yard-line striping courtesy of George P. Toma. Photo by David R. Mellor.

Plate 41: This festive design was done for Ottawa Lynx at Jet Form Park. This is a perfect example of the unlimited options of artistic abilities. Photo courtesy of Peter Webb and Brad Keith.

Plate 42: A pattern used on the Little League World Series Field to add a professional touch to the overall experience for the players and spectators worldwide. Photo courtesy of Little League Baseball.

Plate 43: Patterns are used to enhance the beauty of the infield grass at Daytona Raceway, Florida. Photo courtesy of Daytona Raceway.

Plate 44: Mowing center court at Wimbledon Tennis Club, England. Photo by Gary Prior, courtesy of All Sport Photography.

Plate 45: Here 10-yard sections are mowed light from 5-15 yard lines and dark from 15-25 yard lines and repeated, enabling the 45-45 yard line area to be painted more easily. The machine used mows a path 7 yards wide. Photo by Tom Hauck, courtesy of All Sport Photography.

Plate 46: A "Wave" pattern on the Hinsdale South High School field, Darien, Illinois.
Photo courtesy of Dean Balduff.

Plate 47: Green Bay Packers Lambeau Field. Mowing the 45-45 midfield area all one direction, then alternating light and dark 5-yard sections to the ends of the field gives balance,
and the end zones are easier to paint. Photo courtesy of Rob Anthony.

Plate 48: Even Astroturf® is patterned. Here the nap of the carpet was installed in the opposite direction every 5 yards to create a pattern. Photo courtesy of Aerolist Photographers, Inc.

Plate 49: A tartan plaid theme applied to the lawn of Mark Berman & Son Fine Clothier in Mequon, Wisconsin. Photo by David R. Mellor.

Plate 50: A beautiful checkerboard pattern can enhance the beauty of your home lawn, or show off the professionalism of lawn care operators. Photo courtesy of Simplicity Manufacturing.

Plate 51: Home lawn patterns can be simple to mow, and add significant curb-appeal to your property. Photo courtesy of Simplicity Manufacturing.

Plate 52: Sunburst pattern. This is a nice design to view from an elevated area such as a home or office building. Photo by David R. Mellor.

Plate 53: A traditional checkerboard mowing pattern shown on bluegrass at the Meadow Lands in New Jersey. Photo Courtesy of Rob Davis.

Plate 54: This pattern followed the midfield circle to make a bull's eye design at Soldier Field in Chicago for the 1996 World Cup. Photo Courtesy of John Nolan.

Plate 55: Head groundsman Rob McCullagh and crew prepare for the FA Cup Final Wembley Stadium, England. Photo by Bryan Lynch Lynnphoto, courtesy of Mike Beard, *The Groundsman*, England.

Plate 56: This pattern at the Columbus Crew Stadium is made with all wide lines to form a large checkerboard similar to what you may see in England. Photo Courtesy of Darian Daily.

Plate 57: A creative use of large stripes on this soccer field in Columbus, Ohio. Photo Courtesy of Darian Daily, Columbus Crew.

Plate 58: The mowing lines bend around the midfield circle of the Columbus Crew Stadium. This is similar to the Trail Blazer pattern discussed in chapter 14. Photo Courtesy of Darian Daily.

Plate 59: This picture was taken at The Ohio State Stadium. The diagonal lines help add the appearance of a wider grass area. The lines of different width within the 18-yard penalty shot box adds more detail. Photo Courtesy of Brian Gimbel.

Plate 60: A festive diamond within a diamond pattern on a golf course fairway. This design was created to add visual flair to the 1999, GCSAA Golf Championship played at Rolling Oaks Golf Club, Brooksville, Florida. Photo courtesy of Scott Hollister.

Plate 61: A simple diamond pattern on our own front lawn adds a polished finish to a beautiful landscape. Photo by David R. Mellor.

Plate 62: This diagonal cut does not require continuing a pattern through the pitcher's mound. Photo by David R. Mellor.

Plate 63: Lawn care companies can enhance their work by giving more consideration to applying patterns to industrial property, parks, and home lawns. Photo courtesy of Simplicity Manufacturing.

Plate 64: The Iowa Cubs' AAA baseball field featuring a design they named "the Vortex." As you can see, the outfield grass appears to undulate. Photo courtesy of Luke Yoder.

Chapter 14

PATTERN INSTRUCTIONS

Every design will present challenges, and different strategies may be needed. Once you grasp the basic principles, you'll be able to complete even the most complex designs. Until you've practiced several different techniques and designs, I recommend you start by drawing the design first. This can be done on paper or with your computer. If you are patterning an athletic field, use the handy field diagrams in this book as a guide on which to sketch out your designs. With experience you'll be able to create a pattern as you mow. You'll be able to mow by eye and make your moves by memory. To get started, here are some easy-to-follow patterns with methods and diagrams.

Remember that light stripes are made when the mower travels away from your vantage point and dark stripes are made when the mower moves toward your vantage point. Keep in mind that once you get to the end of a light stripe and turn around, the stripe you just created will look dark because you are now viewing it from the other side of the design.

Checkerboard *(See color plates 2, 18, and 55.)*
A good pattern to start with is the basic checkerboard, a traditional pattern often seen on athletic fields and golf courses. It's easy to implement and looks great.

> **Step 1.** Start your first pass mowing at one side of your site. Then mow (side-by-side) parallel lines, traveling across the turf to the other side. This will produce alternating light and dark stripes. Be sure to overlap your previous mowing stripe with the mower blades to ensure that all the grass is cut.
>
> **Step 2.** Now make a mowing stripe at a 90-degree angle (perpendicular)

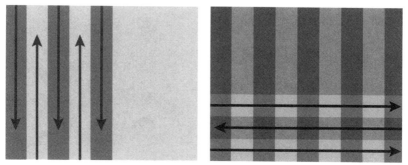

Step 1

Step 2

to your first set of lines. Once you have set your first 90-degree line in the new direction mow parallel lines like you did in Step 1.

These side-by-side mowing stripes will continue across the grass to the other side. Now you have mowed in both directions, establishing the initial checkerboard.

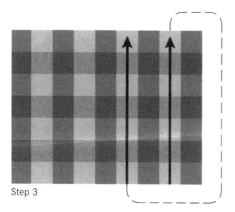

Step 3

Step 3. This step is the key to making your design stand out. Add depth to the design and give the lines more impact by going back over every other stripe of the first direction in the pattern (Step 1). You can perform this task with the cutting blades engaged if you wish. Or disengage the cutting blades, set down the deck or reels, and use only the rollers to bend in the stripes again. Retracing your lines in this manner can be done more quickly when the cutting blades are off, allowing the machine to move in transport mode at a faster ground speed safely.

By skipping every other line you'll bend in only one color (light or dark) of stripe, then transport around to the next line in the same direction as the previous one. Retrace either all the light stripes or all the dark stripes in one direction. This will redefine the checkerboard.

By retracing every other line you will not wipe out or lighten all the previous lines in the other 90-degree line section, you will only redefine the true checkerboard look.

Step 4. Once you have completed Step 3 all that remains is to frame your work of art. Mowing cleanup passes around the outer edge of your site accomplishes this. This will set a frame-like border around the design, and enable you to mow any remaining areas of grass that you might have missed during your turns. These cleanup passes will also remove tire marks from any turns. The number of cleanup passes will vary depending on the site and what you feel achieves a polished finish.

Plaid Design *(See color plates 5 and 6.)*

The plaid design is similar to the checkerboard, but combines lines of different width spaced in a repeating pattern within the design.

Step 1. Start like the checkerboard pattern by making side-by-side parallel mower lines across the grass.

Step 2. When making the crossing stripe lines, start by making single-width or "skinny" line passes side by side on a 90-degree angle from your Step 1 stripes.

Step 3. This is the key to setting your plaid. Drive out on the previous light stripe and then mow coming back beside the last dark return stripe, making a double-wide or "fat" line.

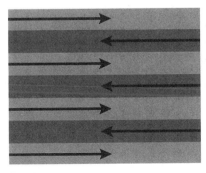
Step 1

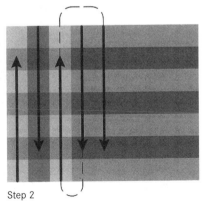
Step 2

Step 4. Repeat Steps 2 and 3, making three more "skinny," normal-width parallel passes with a double-wide fat line until you have covered all the grass.

You can vary your plaid by changing the width of your lines. You can start with one set all of normal width and then change the overlapping crossing stripes, or do both sides with fat and skinny lines in a repeating layout.

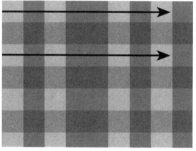

Step 5

Step 5. This step is the key to making your design stand out. Add depth to the design and give the lines more impact by going back over every other stripe of your first direction in the pattern (Step 1). You can perform this task with the cutting blades engaged if you wish. Or disengage the cutting blades, set down the deck or reels, and use only the rollers to bend in the stripes again. Retracing your lines in this manner can be done more quickly when the cutting blades are off, allowing the machine to move in transport mode at a faster ground speed safely.

By skipping every other line, you'll bend in only one color (light or dark) of stripe, then transport around to the next line in the same direction as the previous one. Retrace either all the light stripes or all the dark stripes in one direction. This will redefine the plaid. By retracing every other line you will not wipe out or lighten all the previous lines in the other 90-degree line section, you will only add detail to the plaid.

Step 6. Frame your plaid with cleanup passes. *(See color plates 4, 5, 6, and 7.)*

Small and Big Diamonds *(See color plates 22, 23, and 42.)*

Any diamond pattern is a nice choice for a home lawn or office complex. By setting the angles off of the street line you will create multiple looks for the people passing by. This big and small diamond pattern is made with single "skinny" width lines and double wide "fat" lines. You can decide on the angle of the lines that suit your specific site the best. Just remember not to make them at 90-degree angles (like your checkerboard) to ensure a diamond. If you wish you can use the same concept to make big and small squares.

Step 1

Step 1. This pattern starts by mowing from corner to corner. Do side-by-side parallel lines, then retrace your first line corner-to-corner. Make your next mowing stripe beside the second line you made. This will make it twice as wide. This is a similar process to making the double-wide line in the plaid pattern. However, now you will follow this pattern of one wide stripe away and a double-wide stripe back until you have mowed all of your grass on that side of your turf at this angle.

Step 2. Follow the directions in Step 1 on the side of the uncut grass. Start by mowing out, again on the (original) first corner-to-corner line. Next, follow the procedure of two wide stripes and one thin stripe until you have cut the entire side.

Step 2

Step 3. To establish your crossing lines, use the same angle as before to ensure a true diamond. Once you have determined the proper starting points, follow the same steps as before. Cut the long thin stripe first and create a double-wide stripe beside it. To create the

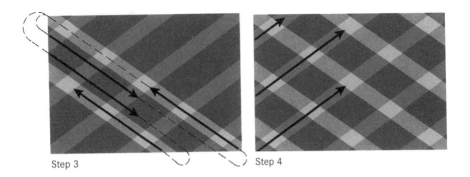

Step 3   Step 4

remaining crossing lines on the other side, go back and start at the long stripe and repeat the single-width line/double-width line pattern across the turf.

Step 4. To make the diamond pattern sparkle, follow the "secret procedure" of retracing only every other line, as described in Step 3 of the checkerboard design example. Retrace the thin lines, and skip the wide lines. This will give extra impact to your pattern and almost make it glow.

Step 5. Frame in your spectacular diamonds with cleanup passes. Once you have successfully created this pattern, you will graduate to the unofficial title of "Diamond Cutter."

Crossing Arches

Crossing arches is an eye-catching pattern that is easier than it looks. It is merely a series of overlapping arches.

Step 1. Start by making a gentle curve across your grass. Make the highest bend of the curve near the midpoint of your site. Once your first line is set, use it as a guide and make your subsequent passes next to it. Follow this line pattern across your site to the other side until the grass is completely cut.

Step 2. Switch sides and make another gentle curve going across the first set of lines on an opposite curve. Try to set a similar bend to the curve of the first angle. Mow, repeating this curve to the other side of the site.

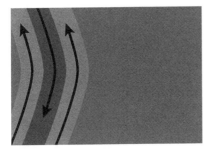

Step 1

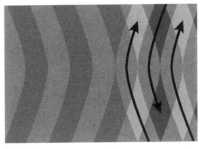

Step 2

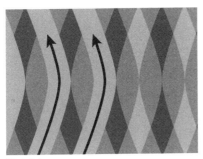

Step 3

Step 3. Add depth to the pattern as described in the earlier examples. Retrace either the dark or light stripes of the first curved passes. Retrace only one of the colors to make the pattern display the detail of these curves. I recommend that you retrace the "light" colored lines beginning with the ones made in step 1, and then redo the "light" lines from step 2 for maximum impact.

Step 4. Frame in the design with cleanup passes and wipe out any tire marks.

The Trail Blazer *(See color plate 8.)*

A design or pattern on clothing, blankets, or rugs often inspires me. This pattern reminds me of the NBA Portland Trailblazers logo. While not identical, the pattern was inspired by the Portland logo. I call it the "Trail Blazer."

Step 1. Use the middle of your site as the point where you will make the dramatic bend or turn in your line. Start with a straight line at an approximate 45-degree angle. Follow this line almost to the middle of the site, then turn toward the opposite angle. While close to it, this is not a quick 90-degree corner turn. Be careful making this bend or turn. If it is too sharp a turn you could damage the turf and the turn angle will be too tight to follow in future passes.

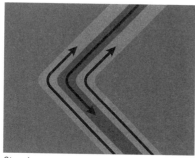

Step 1

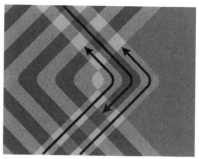

Step 2

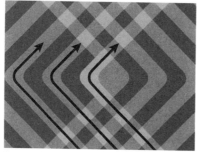

Step 3

Once you have set the first stripe, mow subsequent stripes back and forth, duplicating the original arch until you have worked your way to one side of the site.

Step 2. The next step is to reproduce the arch in a mirror-like fashion. Start this direction like the first set of lines. Use the middle of the area to make the bend in the stripe. This pass should be spaced so that it intersects the first mowed angle, making sure that you do not leave any uncut patches of grass. Working from the middle, continue to reproduce this set of stripes to the other side.

Step 3. Go back and retrace the first angle of stripes by performing the technique used in overlapping curves. Choose either all the dark or all the light stripes to retrace by skipping over the other. You will see how dramatic this step makes your pattern.

The Wave *(See color plates 9 and 10.)*

This pattern comes from a special drawing my daughter did for me with crayons. In the fall of 1996, I was asked to photographically document the different mowing patterns we created at Milwaukee County Stadium for a traveling international art exhibit. Phyllis Lambert, Director of the Canadian Centre for Architecture (CCA), organized the exhibit with design help from the New York architecture firm of Diller and Scofidio. After the baseball season ended in November of 1997, I received a call at home on a Friday night from Diller and Scofidio, asking if I could create a truly unique and arty pattern unlike anything I had ever done. My daughter Catherine, who was six years old at the time, asked who was on the phone. I explained it was the people involved in the art exhibit, and they wanted me to create a really wild pattern. She listened carefully, then went into her room. I started to sketch out possible new design patterns. Approximately a half hour passed before my daughter came back holding something behind her. She asked me to take a look at her drawing. It really grabbed my attention (and not just because of her use of sparkle crayons!) I had never seen a pattern like it. Catherine asked if it would be helpful for the art exhibit. I was excited to give it a try. The next morning my friend Kirt Bakos met me at the stadium

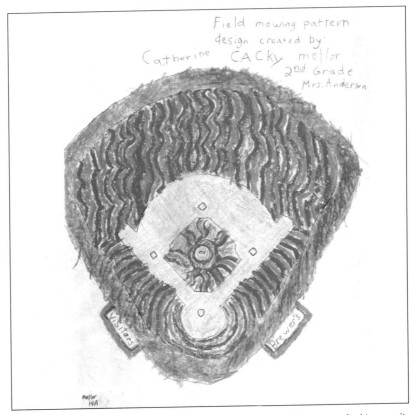

This is a pattern done by my daughter, Catherine. After I saw it, I became excited to mow it.

to help apply it. I was amazed at how easy the design was to install to the turf.

When I sent a series of photographs of "The Wave" to Diller and Scofidio they called the day they received the photographs. At first I was concerned there was a problem with the photos. Then I heard the excitement in their voices and they said how much they enjoyed this clever pattern. They wondered why no one had done this pattern sooner! Of all of the designs, this was the favorite. I told them I was pleased they liked it, but I explained that it was my six-year-old daughter's brainchild. I'm proud to say this pattern is also my personal favorite pattern, and it was displayed in the art exhibit "The American Lawn: Surfaces of Everyday Life."

Following are directions for a fun and easy version of the pattern. It's guaranteed to attract attention. If you are applying it to your home lawn or business complex it is best to angle the pattern across your turf. This will provide interesting views for people driving by in both directions: a wave from one direction and an optical illusion from the other. When you view this design at an angle by looking across the waves, the curves make the surface of the grass appear to undulate. People will do a double take. *(See color plate 11.)*

"Wave" design created with a Simplicity lawn tractor. This design makes the turf appear to undulate, and can be used on everything from home lawns to soccer fields. Photo courtesy of Simplicity Manufacturing.

 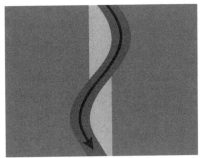

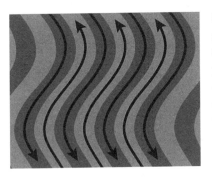

Step 1. Use a straight line as a guide to make your first wavy stripe. Once you make the waves you will erase the straight line. Start the first curved wave at the end of the straight guideline. Like the "Trail Blazer" bend, it is important not to make the curve too tight or it will not reproduce well as you mow further into the design. Make a smooth curved stripe that just crosses over the guideline and then curves back across the guideline. Repeat this gentle curve back and forth across the guideline for the length of your site. Once the first wave is set, duplicate that wavy stripe across your entire site.

Step 2. Frame in the design with cleanup passes.

The Bull's Eye *(See color plate 12 and 54.)*

The Bull's Eye is a relatively easy, yet memorable, design. This pattern is made with concentric circles mown in opposite directions.

Step 1. Think of its name and follow the basic pattern. So that the pattern has balance, start in an area near the middle of your site and work your way out. Frame in a circle by making a clockwise stripe framing in a circle, then the next circular stripe in the opposite direction or counterclockwise. Continue to duplicate these circles as you make your way to the edge of your site.

Step 1

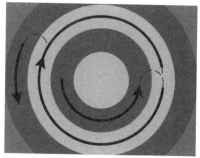

Step 2

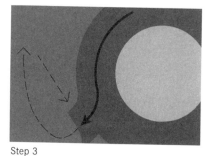

Step 3

Step 2. The key to the visual impact of this pattern is where you make the turns to start the next circle in the opposite direction. Determine where the main viewing location of the pattern will be, then imagine your site as the face of a clock. Each subsequent pass in your pattern should erase the previous turn marks, but it is helpful to make your turns at the 2-4 o'clock and 8-10 o'clock positions, as they relate to the main viewing location.

As discussed in Chapter 9, be careful making your turns. Execute slow, wide turns and then back up and align the mower beside the existing circle for a starting position for the next pass. Remember to not turn the steering wheel too quickly, which may cause the tires to grab and tear the grass. If you are not careful, quick movement will damage the grass. This type of damage can add up quickly and force you to change the pattern sooner than you planned.

Step 3. Frame in the design with cleanup passes.

Logos

Many logos can be created through mowing patterns. A well-done mowing logo is easier on the grass than a painted logo and can be changed or removed much more quickly and easily.

#19 (*See color plate 13.*)

On May 29, 1994 the Milwaukee Brewers retired Hall of Fame short-stop Robin Yount's uniform number. On a challenge from a ground crew member we created a #19 pattern on our infield. It was our thank you to Robin for being a great player, a special person, and a friend to the grounds crew. Making the circle top of the 9 was challenging. We soon realized that if we made a circle, only half of it would be visible. Because of the way the grass blades bend when making a full circle, half toward and half away from the viewing area, the circle became half dark arch and half light arch. (*See color plate 13.*)

There is an interesting twist to the #19 pattern. It took two days to learn how to make it properly. After the first day I received a call from Tom Haudricourt, the Baseball writer for the *Milwaukee Journal/Sentinel*. He had heard through the igrapevine that we were patterning the #19 on the infield in honor of Yount. He asked if it was true and I told him that we were working on it, but that it wasn't finished. I didn't want to say it was a sure thing. Then we talked a little more about the details.

The next morning I went to work early and started on the infield design at sunrise. I would put part of the nine in, view it from the upper deck of the stadium, then come down and make adjustments. At about 8:00 A.M. I noticed several employees looking at the field. One stopped by the front row railing and called to me. He said it was a nice touch to put Robin's number on the grass. His comments took me by surprise. I was shocked how much he knew about what we were doing and asked how he knew so much. He said he had read about it in the paper that morning. The pressure was really on now to make it work.

The Vice President of Stadium Operations, Gabe Paul Jr., came down to the field at 8:30 A.M. He said he too had seen the mention of the #19 in the paper. He said in very plain terms that now that the public knew what we were trying to do it had better work! I am proud to say we did create the #19 pattern and received a great deal of positive feedback.

Step 1. First, using a triplex reel mower we mowed the infield grass several times from home plate to second base to create a light background and remove a previous pattern that was visible from behind home plate. The numbers were installed with a walk-behind reel mower, the cutting blades were disengaged, and the rollers bent in the design.

Step 2. We measured the size of the number, centered it, and set and pinned line strings.

Step 3. The # 1 was easy. We started from the third base line following the light-colored bend in the grass to the top of the "1" beside the line strings. At the top, we turned around and went back on the opposite side of the line string, making a dark stripe to the bottom of the number. Going back against the bend of the light-colored turf made a dark, vivid stripe. At the base of the string we turned to the right and went back up to the top of the line string, retracing the light stripe.
Step 4. At the top of the string we turned to the right, moved over one mower width, and traveled down to the base of the number one, making the dark stripe double wide. At the base, we carefully turned to the left and went back up beside the dark line, framing it in with a light stripe. The number one was then set. To etch in the number you can repeat each of these steps.

Step 5. We followed the same steps to make the straight line in the #9.

Step 6. To solve the problem of the circle part of the 9 showing half light/half dark, we first offset each half arch by the width of our walk-behind reel mower (21 inches). Then we connected a letter "C" and a reverse letter "C" to make the circle look complete. If you look closely you may be able to see this, but because each arch is framed in like the straight lines in the design, they appear bold and connected. Each arch is a double-wide dark stripe framed in with a single-width light arch. From a distance the two letter "C's" appear to be one continuous dark circle.

Now you know the "secret" approach to making a circle appear to be the same color within a design. You can use the same principles of framing in wide stripes with thin stripes to create other logos and designs. (*See color plate 14.*)

"M" is for... (*See color plate 15.*)

The "M" shown here was the Brewers' hat insignia of a few years ago. I also liked it because it is my last initial. The last name of the young man who helped me install this pattern started with "W". Viewed from the opposite direction he claimed it was his initial, but of course we told everyone that it was for Wisconsin.

Step 1. We measured off seven equal sections. The middle section was made light to contrast well with the dark "M". In the remaining sections we alternated the mowing direction of each section to result in the light and dark sunburst effect.

Step 2. The area behind second base, in short center field, is close enough to be clearly visible. To center and balance the logo, we remeasured the center section to find its midpoint. The sides of the "M" were then measured and set with a line string, then the slants to make the middle part of the "M" were set with a line string. Each line string was pulled tight and pinned at each end, then pins were added between to ensure a straight line.

Step 3. We installed the logo with a walk-behind reel mower, disengaged the reels, and used only the roller to bend in the design. To make double-wide stripes, we started by transporting on the light stripe to the top of the "M" on the third base side. Then we turned and followed the line string to the bottom of the "M". We utilized the same framing process to the main stripe as in the #19 logo. We framed in the dark stripe by going back to the top of the "M" directly beside it on the outside of the logo.

Step 4. Next, we moved over to make a double-wide dark stripe for the other leg of the "M", and framed in that side as we did the first, again on the outside of the logo.

Step 5. To define the left slant of the "M", we turned right and followed the slanted line string to the point in the middle. We then turned right again and followed the line string back to where we started this step (framing in the slanted dark line on that side). We then crossed over the dark line just far enough to turn right, and made a double-wide slanted line. We followed it to the middle, turned left, and traveled back to the top of the "M", framing in that side. We had the left half of the "M" done—double-wide dark lines framed in by a single-width light stripe.

Step 6. To define the other side, we retraced the previous dark inside slanted line. At the middle point we went back up the other slant on the outside of the bottom, making the frame-in line to the other slant.

Step 7. At the top of the slant we turned left and went back down beside the framing stripe we had just made. At the midpoint, again we carefully turned left and traveled back up, retracing the framing stripe.

Step 8. We followed the directions in Steps 3 and 4 to create the other leg of the letter "M" and finish the design.

Advanced Examples *(See color plates 29, 30, and 31.)*

These examples are of more advanced patterns. Extra care must be taken when creating patterns that require changing one pattern within another. The turn areas or transition points from section to section are critical. These transition areas can show wear very quickly. Each pattern will have its own specific challenges. These wear areas should be considered and addressed in advance so that when you apply the pattern the grass will be better prepared to withstand the

Advanced patterns like this one take lots of preparation and practice. Photo by Joe Picciolo, courtesy of the Milwaukee Brewers Baseball Club.

The home of the Appleton, Wisconsin, Timber Rattlers. Photo courtesy of Chad Huss.

A complex and visually stimulating pattern at the Oakland Alameda Stadium. Photo courtesy of the Oakland A's Baseball Club and Clay Wood.

additional wear. See Chapter 9, Preventing Traffic and Wear, for more in-depth information on preventive wear maintenance practices and how to hide damage if it occurs. Be sure to lift the reels or mowing deck at the end of each pass before making any turns. This will minimize the bending of the grass blades and will not interfere with the lines in your next section. Your main concern should be possible compaction of the root zone and turf damage caused by the tires of your machine due to repetitive turning in the limited space.

Creating designs with walk-behind reel mowers and hand rollers presents different challenges than when using machines with tires. Because you're traveling on a roller, the entire surface of the roller is on the grass when you make the turns. Follow the basic slow, wide turn technique. Where I have seen damage most often is when someone tries to realign the roller. Do not wiggle the machine, make big shifts, or spin the roller while lining up for the next stripe. Doing so can not only crush the blades of the grass, but it can also bruise and damage the crown of the turfgrass plant. This damage can be seen as it occurs but it tends to become more apparent during the following days. This damage can be slow to heal, and once it happens it can limit the number of times you can do that pattern. It may be necessary to change to another design to reduce the stresses and give the turfgrass time to recover.

It's a good idea to practice many turns in difficult-to-see areas to develop a better feel for your machine and learn the proper techniques for your design. You don't want to cause damage when starting a pattern and then not be able to finish. These advanced patterns are well worth the extra care you must give the grass, but I don't recommend them for beginners. As you gain experience and advance through the different types of patterns you will be more prepared to handle the hurdles you will face when developing peerless patterns like these.

Lining up the stripes of matching designs can be tricky on complex patterns with sections of different design. Place the mower where you think it should be, then check the alignment by stepping back 20 to 30 feet to gain perspective. Make adjustments if necessary, then check the alignment from the coordinating section. Continue the process until the mower is in the correct location to begin the stripe.

By practicing the techniques in the previous examples you will have the basic skills and knowledge to tackle more advanced patterns, whether they are original or copied designs. Before long you will be able to create your own gallery of "Lawn Art."

Maintaining Designs

Once you have an established pattern with the crossing stripes you want, you will not have to mow both crossing angle directions each time. Mow the entire turf area back and forth following one of the angles that is already visible. Then perform the "every other stripe" system on the other established angle. This will eliminate mowing twice and save time.

An alternative method: Mow the first mowing angle today, then roll every other line on the opposite angle. On the next mowing, mow the angle where before you only rolled the lines, and then only roll every other stripe on the other angle. During subsequent mowings, alternate which set of angles you mow and which you only roll.

Recording Your Work

Photograph your patterns and create a reference file so you can refer to them later. Photographs are also a great tool to learn from. Be sure to photograph all your patterns—the great ones, and the ones that didn't quite work. See Chapter 15, Photographing Your Lawn Art, for tips on photography.

Chapter 15

PHOTOGRAPHING YOUR LAWN ART

Capturing a good picture can make all the difference in how your pattern is remembered. Take your time when photographing your work. After all, you have put a lot of tender loving care into your pattern. You want the picture or slide to reflect that effort. Invest some time speaking with experts at a photography store. Explain what you're photographing and ask for guidelines to make your photographs "picture perfect." Since your subject is grass, ask what brand of film they recommend to bring out the green and blue colors rather than the red colors. I like to use Fuji slide film to enhance the green grass patterns.

In this case a picture is worth ten thousand words. Let pictures of your patterns speak of your creativity. Developing a portfolio of pictures of your patterns can be a powerful resource. During the process of writing this book, I contacted many talented colleagues and asked to use photographs of their work in the book. Some declined because they either did not take pictures or the photos didn't turn out as they had hoped. Several stated they were planning on making time to document their patterns in the future. Documenting your patterns can be a useful reference when you're trying to remember the details of a favorite design. Photos will save you time when you start on a pattern that you thought you remembered, only to realize that you don't. Photographs of your patterns can be displayed to express your pride and craftsmanship. Feature them in the marketing of your lawn care business, or even when selling your home to show the buyer the curb appeal of your property. If you work in turf management, quality photographs of your work can remind your supervisors you're willing to provide the extra effort needed to go beyond just cutting the grass.

I feel it's important to photograph not only your favorite or best patterns but all of them. Keep a loaded camera and an extra roll of film handy so you can take a photograph whenever the opportunity arises. Part of being successful is learning from your mistakes. Being able to compare your different patterns side by side in photos will provide you with the opportunity to better evaluate each of them. By reviewing the photographs you'll be able to scrutinize each pattern and improve on it in your future creations. Sometimes there are attractive parts of a pattern within a whole that just didn't turn out. Pictures help me learn from the good and not-so-good sections of a pattern. I have combined sections I liked from several different patterns to create a completely new one. It was easier and quicker to install since I had already performed parts of it before.

I've learned the hard way—taking what I thought were good pictures of a pattern, and then changing the design. When the film came back from processing I was disappointed to see that the pictures didn't turn out. But I had already changed my pattern and lost the opportunity to document it. I quickly realized that I needed to learn more about photography, and therefore I take numerous pictures of the same pattern in hopes that I get one that captures the pattern well.

Though you don't need an expensive camera, a quality camera will provide you with better images. Consider how you're going to use your images before you buy film. Slide film will usually reproduce into photographs or other slides better than print films. Try to match the film speed with the conditions in which you're going to shoot the film. The higher the film speed the lower the available light can be.

The time of day when you photograph your patterns has a direct relationship to the outcome. Have the sun behind you, shining over your shoulder, when taking the picture. If the sun is directly above or you are shooting into the sun, the highlights of your pattern will be washed out. Taking a picture on cloudy days, or following a rain, can add interesting diffused light to your patterns. Before taking a picture, choose the best vantage point to take it from. Don't just take it from a location because it's convenient. Explore interesting perspectives that can add drama to your photographs. The eye-catching elements within patterns can include the strong contrasts of the light and dark stripes. The obvious shapes within a pattern work by attracting a viewer's eye. You can seize people's attention by making them think about or wonder how you did it. If you have water available, lightly sprinkle or mist water over your grass before taking a picture. The water droplets that form on the grass blades will enliven the contrasts between the light and dark sections and make your pattern almost glow. The effect will heighten the boldness of the lines.

Special effects can be used in a multitude of ways to heighten the atmosphere of your photos. You can be creative with a few accessories, such as different sizes of lenses, different filters, and different types of film. (*See color plates 16 and 17.*)

Chapter 16

THREE CHALLENGING SITUATIONS

Dealing with Mother Nature is a major part of my job. She influences what, when, and how we do our work. I want to share with you three amusing and unique experiences. I believe it's important to hope for the best, but always be prepared to deal with the worst.

When It Rains, It Pours

On August 6, 1997, Milwaukee was hit by one of its largest rainstorms in 100 years. The Brewers were in the middle of a home stand against the Kansas City Royals. After the previous night's game the grounds crew put the tarp over the infield because we were expecting rain overnight. Little did we know that this rain would be a "Storm of the Century"-the second such storm in 11 years for Milwaukee. In 1986 Milwaukee County Stadium flooded after a torrential storm.

At 4:00 A.M. that Saturday I was jolted awake when lightning lit up the room, followed by an eardrum-splitting clap of thunder. I quickly tuned the TV to the Weather Channel. On the radar screen a long red blob spread over Milwaukee. As the radar went into motion it showed how a portion of the storm had already passed the city, and how much of it was still over Milwaukee. I saw an even larger storm area tracking straight for downtown. The storm conditions we had that day are called a "training effect." These conditions are caused when numerous storms combine and travel over one area like a train following railroad tracks. I looked outside. My yard was starting to flood. There was a game scheduled for 7:05 that evening. I quickly got dressed.

A friend was visiting, and I woke him to say I was going to work to check on the field because of the storm. He was scheduled to drive back to Denver that day and decided to get an early start. He followed me to the highway in an absolute downpour. On the interstate we had oncoming traffic traveling north in the southbound lanes. A quarter mile ahead I saw a long traffic jam. Luckily we were able to turn around, go back to our original exit, and try alternative routes. On a normal Saturday morning it takes me about fifteen minutes to drive to the stadium. On this morning it took 21/2 hours, winding through flooded streets and detouring around closed ones. When I arrived at 7:00 A.M. the field had about 3 inches of water covering the warning track, and the first 50 feet of the outfield grass all around was submerged as well. Despite being awakened so early, my friend continued on safely to Denver and was glad he left when he did.

At 9:00 A.M. the rain was still coming down in buckets. Sixty percent of the outfield grass was now under water.

At 10:30 A.M. the rain finally stopped, but most of the field was flooded. A local TV helicopter reporter checking the city for flood damage flew over the stadium. She reported, "At least County Stadium isn't flooded too much. I can still see the green grass through the water." The "green grass" she reported was grass clippings floating on top of three feet of water.

We were lucky we didn't have more water on the field. It could have been worse. Miller Park, the Brewers' state-of-the-art stadium, is located in the parking lot between County Stadium and the river that overflowed. At that time the sublevel of the new stadium was being excavated and the massive hole filled with more than six feet of water. Miller Park, in its infancy of construction, made a significant contribution that day.

Natural disasters, like this flood, can cause major headaches. Photo by Joe Picciolo, courtesy of the Milwaukee Brewers Baseball Club

A 1997 photo of the flooded construction site at Miller Park in Milwaukee Wisconsin. Housing six feet of standing water, this construction project helped save the field at Milwaukee County Stadium. Photo courtesy of Joe Vopal

Unfortunately, the August 6th game was canceled due to flooding. With thorough communication and teamwork, the grounds crew, along with outside help, was able to make the field safe and playable for the next day's game. We also hired Milwaukee's Channel 12 Television's traffic helicopter to assist in returning the field to playing condition. Their pilot hovered the helicopter inside the stadium 12 feet above the ground for six hours. A grounds crewmember rode inside the helicopter with a two-way radio to communicate with the pilot, directing them to wet locations. The strong downdraft created by the helicopter's turning blades dried and fluffed the grass. It was like using a giant blow dryer.

A Friend of Pepé Le Pew

In the middle of an inning during a game against the Toronto Blue Jays, a skunk burrowed out from underneath the outfield bleachers. The umpires were forced to stop play. We were very careful not to frighten the skunk into spraying. The gentle encouragement of six grounds crew members herded the skunk toward the bullpen gate in left-center field. When the skunk realized the gate was open and it was welcome to leave, it ran off the field, out the back of the bullpen, and under a large trash compactor behind the scoreboard. After the brief delay, play resumed and everyone breathed a fresh air sigh of relief.

The following morning at 9 A.M. sharp my phone rang. It was an extremely upset lady from Los Angeles who had been misinformed that the skunk had been injured. Despite her creating quite a stink, I assured her that we absolutely did not harm the skunk and relayed what had actually happened.

This is for the birds!

At Milwaukee County Stadium we handle any situation with animals with extreme care. In 1993 after a Paul McCartney concert we subcontracted the service of a solid deep-tine Verti-Drain (turf aerator to relieve the compaction of the soil caused by the concert. Because of time constraints the aerating was done overnight. The same night I installed my first truly unique pattern on the infield (explained in Chapter 1, Introduction).

That night thousands of insects hatched from a group of trees near the stadium. Being insects, they were drawn to the stadium lights, which were on while the work was being done. When the lights were turned off at sunrise the insects settled on the field grass. An hour later I saw a dozen seagulls land on the outfield, eat some bugs, then fly away. County Stadium is about three miles from Lake Michigan, which is home to many seagulls. It's not unusual to see gulls in the County Stadium parking lot after events, but to see them on the field was unique. An hour later a hundred seagulls descended onto the field, devoured some bugs, and then flew away again. They must have told their fiends because after another hour passed hundreds of seagulls returned to feed on the bugs. The seagulls were everywhere.

At 8:30 A.M. my boss, Gary, arrived. We discussed what we could do to get the birds to leave. Suddenly at 9:00 A.M. the birds flew away and we figured we were finally in the clear.

Since I had worked all the previous night I went home at 1:00 P.M. That evening about 7:00 P.M. my phone rang. It was Gary. "Are you listening to the game?" he asked. "No, I was about to go to sleep," I replied. He said, "They're back!" It looked like a scene from Alfred Hitchcock's *The Birds*. Hundreds of seagulls were circling the stadium lights, getting close to landing on the field at game time.

Of all teams, the New York Yankees were in town. The game was played, but the Yankees were very concerned about the gulls. A few years earlier, in Toronto, Yankee outfielder Dave Winfield, while playing catch, accidentally hit a flying seagull with a ball and killed it. The

Yankees found out the hard way that the seagull is covered by the Migratory Bird Protection Act. A violation of the Act, which prohibits harming them, is punishable by law. Dave Winfield was arrested that night in Canada. The umpires informed us that the birds could not interfere with play or the Brewers would have to forfeit the next night's game if the birds were still a problem.

The insects that had originally drawn the birds onto the field were gone. But the birds had started a habit that now had to be broken. Through quick research we became aware of the implications of the Migratory Bird Protection Act. We promptly called the Department of Natural Resources (DNR) for guidance on how to handle the gulls. The DNR said the birds could not be harmed, but could be harassed. We needed to make the field an unwelcome environment.

The next morning the Milwaukee County Sheriff's Department's bomb squad ignited special loud explosives on the field to scare the birds away. After the initial noise, the birds flew away, but they returned to the field within five minutes. The DNR provided us with track starter pistols with blanks and specially fitted pyrotechnics to scare the seagulls. These "fireworks" worked well but could not be used during a game. We harassed the birds with irrigation sprinklers and loud music from the stadium's sound system. A company that had seen the bird problem on TV was kind enough to try to help. They delivered a special 5-foot-by-12-foot speaker that emitted high-pitched sounds that were supposed to make the birds uncomfortable and leave. Unfortunately, none these tactics were successful.

A friend of mine, John Turner, suggested we do what some golf courses do to scare geese away: employ birddogs. My wife's boss then, Nic Ehr, was active in the Wisconsin Waterfowl Association, so I contacted him for a referral to members whose dogs were trained well enough to help us. We wanted bird dogs because they are taught to have "soft mouths." Should they catch a bird, the dogs would not harm it, but only bring it back to the handler for release. (For the record, no birds were caught or harmed.) Nic supplied us with the names of ten owners and we arranged a "tryout camp" to select the dogs that worked the best.

There are two minutes between innings in a Major League Baseball game. The dogs had to be trained well enough to run after the birds for 90 seconds and then return to their handlers on a hand command. Voice commands or whistles would not be possible in the stadium with music blasting and fans yelling. Six dogs were selected to help us. Two of my favorites were Sarge and Gus. The two dogs employed the first night were a big hit. In the left field and right field corners a grounds crew member sat with a dog and its handler in the front row of the stands. Between innings the dogs had a blast running after the birds. Everyone liked them except the birds. By the fourth game the dogs were so popular they were introduced on the scoreboard along with the Brewer's starting line up. Two dogs worked each of the remaining games in that 15-game home stand. They performed to the highest level.

These dogs were so well trained that after Sarge's owner was injured in a car accident it was decided that I could be taught his command signals and he could stay with me for the rest of the home stand. I couldn't have been happier. I love dogs.

One dog even received a standing ovation, although it wasn't for its chasing ability. After cruising for gulls between innings, the dog decided it had to go (not leave the field, but go). It squatted not far from the left fielder and did its business, leaving a pile. The crowd erupted in laughter and applause. Sometimes your solution to a problem needs a solution. While we had hoped this wouldn't happen, we were prepared with a bucket and shovel.

Even though the bugs—the seagull's food source—were gone after the first day, the seagulls' landing habit was hard to break. Even after the 15-game home stand the seagulls continued to show up like clockwork, arriving at sunrise, leaving at 9:00 A.M., and returning again at 7:00 P.M. We had to be there at sunrise and sunset to harass them. Finally, after an exhausting four weeks, they left. I now have a new perspective on "Jonathan Livingston Seagull."

Beware of dog! Troy Smith and me taking care of some business, when the game was interrupted by our bird-dog, Gus, who received a standing ovation when he was done.

Photo courtesy of Kirt Bakos

Chapter 17
TURFGRASS FACTOIDS

America has over 50,000 square miles of lawn occupying more area than any single crop, including wheat, corn or tobacco.

Annually Americans spend more than $30 billion on turfgrass. In 1992-1993, Americans spent $750 million on 400 million pounds of grass seed.

10 times more chemical pesticides are used per acre by homeowners than by farmers.

Above Ground
- Grass plants are 70 to 80% water
- Grass clippings are 90% water
- Grass clippings contain 4% nitrogen, 2% potassium and 0.5% phosphorus
- A 10,000 square foot lawn will contain:
  6 grass plants per square inch
  850 plants per square foot
  8.5 million plants total

Below Ground
- 90% of the weight of grass is in its roots
- A single grass plant has 387 miles of root
- There are 329,000 miles of root per square foot
- 3 billion miles of roots in a 10,000 square foot lawn
- Turfgrass sod is a superior form of erosion control, with tests documenting:

    A dense lawn is 6 times more effective than a wheat
    field and 4 times betterthan a hayfield at absorbing rainfall.

Sediment losses from sodded areas will be 8 to 15 times less than for tested man-made erosion control materials and 10 times less than for a straw covered area.

Runoff from a sodded area will take 28 to 46 times longer than for five popular erosion control materials.

A 50 by 50 foot lawn (2,500 square feet) releases enough oxygen for a family of four, while absorbing carbon dioxide, hydrogen fluoride and perosyacetyle nitrate.

Chapter 18

RESOURCES

Associations

American Nursery & Landscape	www.anla.org
American Pathological Society Plant Pathology	www.scisoc.org
American Seed Trade Association	www.amseed.com
American Society of Agronomy	www.agronomy.org
American Society of Golf Course Architects	www.golfdesign.org
Australian Golf Course Superintendents Association	www.agcsa.com.au
Associated Landscape Contractors	www.alca.org
British and International Golf Greenkeepers Association	www.bigga.co.uk
Canadian Seed Trade Association	www.cdnseed.org
Chamber of Commerce	www.uschamber.org
Club Managers Association of America	www.club-mgmt.com
Crop Science Society of America	www.agronomy.org
Garden Writers Association of America	www.hygexpo.com/gwaa
Greenkeeper Verband Deutschland *(German)*	www.golf-infos.de/

Golf Course Builders Association of America   www.gcbaa.org

Golf Course Superintendents   www.gcsaa.org
Professional association with Association of America mission of serving its members and advancing their profession

International Turfgrass Society (ITSWEB)   gnv.ifas.ufl.edu/~itsweb/

Irrigation Association   www.irrigation.org

National Gardening Association   www.garden.org

National Golf Foundation   www.ngf.org

National Golf Course Owners Association   www.ngcoa.com

Noer Foundation   www.noerfoundation.org
A tax deductible, not-for-profit foundation established in 1959, dedicated to financial support of scientific research in turfgrass

Outdoor Power Equipment Institute   opei.mow.org/Admin/index.html

Professional Golfers Association Online   www.pgaonline.com

Professional Grounds Management Society   www.pgms.org

Professional Lawn Care Association of America   www.plcaa.org

Royal Canadian Golf Association   www.rcga.org

Small Business Legislative Council   www.sblc.org

Soil and Water Conservation Society   www.infonet.net/showcase/swcs/

Sports Turf Managers Association   www.aip.com/stma

Turfgrass Association of Australia   www.tgaa.asn.au/

Turfgrass Growers Association   www.turfgrass.co.uk

Turfgrass Producers International	www.turfgrasssod.org

Turfgrass Resource Center (TRC)   www.turfgrasssod.org/trc
Turfgrass Producers International   Toll Free: 800-405-8873
1855-A Hicks Road   Phone: 847-705-9898
Rolling Meadows, Ill 60008   FAX: 847-705-8347

Non-profit site provided by the TPI Association for anyone wanting information about turfgrass and sod

United States Croquet Association   www.ontheweb.ccm/usca/home.html

United States Golf Association   www.usga.org/green/index.html
(Green Section)

Water Environment Federation   www.wef.org

Associations, Turf-State/Regional/Local

Colorado Sports Turf Managers Association   www.cstma.org

Florida Turfgrass Association   www.ftga.org

Georgia Turfgrass Foundation Trust   www.turfgrass.org

Illinois Turfgrass Foundation   www.turf.uiuc.edu/itf/itf.html

Kansas Turfgrass Foundation   www.oznet.ksu.edu/dp_hfrr/turf/

Landscape Ontario Home Page   www.hort-trades.com

Michigan Turfgrass Foundation   www.michiganturf.org

Nebraska Turfgrass Foundation   hort.unl.edu/ntf

New Jersey Nursery & Landscape Association   www.njnla.com

New Jersey Turfgrass Foundation   www.njturfgrass.org/foundatn.html

New York State Turfgrass Association   www.nysta.org

Ontario Turfgrass Research Foundation   www.uoguelph.ca/GTI/guest/otrf.htm

Sod Growers Association of Mid-America	www.turf.uiuc.edu/midwest sod/ sod-producers.html
Southern California Turfgrass Foundation	turfgrassfoundation.org
Southern California Turfgrass Council	www.turfcouncil.org
SW Turfgrass Association	www.cahe.nmsu.edu/cahe/ces/yard
Texas Turfgrass Association	www.texasturf.com/index.htm

Associations, Environmental

American Rivers Society	www.igc.apc.org/rms
Audubon Cooperative Sanctuary Program for Golf Courses	greensection/audubon.html
Care for the Environment While Caring for Your Lawn	www.magicouncil.org/carefor.htm
E.A.G.L.E.	www.cp.duluth.mn.us/~lakes/eagle.html
Environmental Defense Fund	www.edf.org
Environmental World Wide Web Site	www.webcom.co./~staber/welcome.html
Greenlink	www.greenlink.org
National Institute for the Environment	www.inhs.uiue.edu/niewww/cnie.html
National Parks and Conservation Association	www.npca.org
Pesticide Degradation in Golf	www.ianr.unl.edu/ianr/
Course Fairway Conditions	pat/thelabel/lab95sep.htm
Reducing Emissions from Lawn Care Equipment	www.epa.gov/OMSWWW/lg-tips.htm

Diseases

Biological Control of Dollar Spot Disease in Turf	www.uoguelph.ca/Research/crd tech/boland.html
Bipolaris & Exserohilum (Helminthosporium)	aggiehorticulture.tamu.edu/ plantanswers/turf/publications
Brownpatch	aggie-horticulture.tamu.edu/ plantanswers/turf/publications
Common Southern Diseases	http://cygnus.tamu.edu/Texlab/tpdh.html
Dollar Spot	aggie-horticulture.tamu.edu/ plantanswers/turf/publications
Extension Plant Pathology	www.ksu.ksu.edu/plantpath/ extension/facts
Fusarium Blight	aggie-horticulture.tamu.edu/ plantanswers/turf/publications
GTI Bulletin Board-Diseases	http://131.104.114.8/wwwboard/ tmbb15.htm
IPM Prescriptions	www.efn.org/~ipmpa/diseases.html
Major Diseases of Turf Grasses in Western Canada	www.agric.gov.ab.ca/pests/ diseases/turfgras.html
Plant Dictionary(OSU)	www.hcs.ohio-state.edu/plants.html
Plant Disease Management Information	etcs.ext.missouri.edu/agebb/pdmgt/ index.htm
Plant Health Services	www.wisc.edu/plhealthser
Pythium Blight	aggie-horticulture.tamu.edu plantanswers/turf/publications/

| St. Augustine Decline | aggie-horticulture.tamu.edu |
| | plantanswers/turf/publications |

| Texas Plant Disease Handbook | cygnus.tamu.edu |

| The Plant Pathology Internet Guide Book | www.ifgb.uni-hannover.de/extern/ppigb |

Equipment/Suppliers

| Cyberlawn USA | www.mow.org |

| Resource site for turf Industry | turfzone.com |

| International Lawn, Garden and Power Equipment Expo | www.expo.mow.org |

Irrigation

| Lawn Genie | www.lawngenie.com |
| Div. of The Toro Company | Phone: 800-231-5117 |

| Hunter Irrigation | www.hunterirrig.com |
| San Marcos, CA | Phone: 760-744-5240 |

| Rain Bird Consumer Products Mfg. | www.rianbird.com |
| San Diego, CA | Phone: 619-661-4200 |

| Irrigation Association | www.irrigation.org/ia |
| | Phone: 703-573-3551 |

| Water Quality and Golf Course | www.ces.ncsu.edu/TurfFiles/ |
| Superintendents | pubs/wqwm154.html |

| Water Quality and Professional | www.ces.ncsu.edu/TurfFiles/ |
| Turf Managers | pubs/wqwm156.html |

| Water Wise Council of Texas | www.waterwisetexas.org |

Tips on water conservation

Lawn Rollers

Gandy   www.gandy.net
                                         800-443-2476

Mowers, Lawn and Garden/Rotary

Ariens Co.   www.ariens.com
Brillon, WI   Phone: 800-678-5443

Ferris Industries   www.ferrisindustries.com
Minnsville, NY   www.derbymowers.com
A mower with rollers made by Ferris is the Derby Stallion Phone: 800-933-6175

Simplicity Manufacturing, Inc.   www.simplicitymfg.com
500 N Spring Street   Phone: 414-284-8669
Port Washington, WI   or 414-284-8670
*The only company that manufactures a full line of lawn and garden tractors and riding mowers available
with full-width rollers necessary to stripe your lawn*

Reel Mowers, Push

American Lawn Mower Company   Phone: 800-633-1501
Great States Corporation

Husqvarna   www.husqvarna.com
Charlotte, NC   Phone: 704-597-5000

Reel Mowers, Power

Alroh Turf Machinery Services P/L   Phone: 9201-9000
Osborn Park, Western Australia

Atco-Qualcast LTD.   www.atco.co.uk
Suffolk, England   Phone: 01449-742000
Lawnmower manufacturer since 1921

McLane Mfg.   www.mclanemower.com
Paramount, CA   Phone: 562-633-8158

National Mower Co.   www.nationalmower.com
St. Paul, MN   Phone: 651-646-4079

Jacobsen Manufacturing
Racine, WI

www.jacobsen.textron.com
Phone: 414-637-6711

John Deere
Moline. IL

www.deere.com
Phone: 800-537-8233

Sabre lawn tractors, yard and garden tractors, riding mowers

Professional Lawn Equipment
Ferndale, South Africa

www.lawnmower.co.za
Phone: 793-1391

The Toro Company
Bloomington, MN

www.toro.com/
Phone: 800-348-2424

Tools/Lawn Care Products

Minuteman Parker
Addison, IL

www.minutemanintl.com
Phone: 630-627-6901

A.M. Leonard, Inc.
Piqua, OH

Phone: 800-543-8955

Gardener's Supply Company
Burlington, VT

www.gardeners.com/gardeners
Phone: 800-863-1700

Gardens Alive
Lawrenceburg, IN

www.gardens-alive.com
Phone: 812-537-8650 or 812-537-8651

Restore your lawn and garden the organic way with all-natural fertilizers and pest control

Harmony Farm Supply
3244 Gravenstein Hwy.
North Sebastopol, CA 95472

www.harmonyfarm.com
Phone: 707-823-9125
FAX 707-823-1734

Organic farm and garden supply

The Scott's Company

www.scottscompany.com

Advice for the homeowner wanting a beautiful lawn, including seeding, watering, and mowing; also, answers to problems from weeds to insects

Mellinger's Online Garden Catalog
Lima, OH

www.mellingers.com
Phone: 800-321-7444

Extension Bulletins (Miscellaneous)

Extension and Outreach (U of IL)	www.turf.uiuc.edu/extension/extension.html
Landscape CAT Alerts (MSU)	www.msue.msu.edu/msue/imp/modc1/masterc1.html
Turfgrass Extension Articles (Rutgers)	www.cook.rutgers.edu/~turf/extension.html
Turfgrass Extension Publications (U of KY)	www.uky.edu/Agriculture/ukturf/pubs.htm
Turfgrass Management) and Use (Texas A&M	aggie-horticulture.tamu.edu plantanswers/turf/turf.html
Turf Tips (Purdue)	shadow.agry.purdue.edu/agronomy/turf/turftips.htm

Fertility

Common Turfgrass Fertilizers	www.scgt.oz.au/ferts.html
Fertilizer Spreaders	aggie-horticulture.tamu.edu plantanswers/turf/fertsprd.html
GTI Bulletin Board-Fertility	http://131.104.114.8/wwwboard/tmbb8.htm
Organic fertilizers	www.btw.com/garden_archive/3frtlzr3.html
Salt Indexes of Turf Fertilizers	www.psupena.psu.edu:70/0%24d%2028801205

Government, United States

National Turfgrass Evaluation Program	hort.unl.edu/ntep
United States Department of Agriculture	www.usda.gov
Extension Agencies	www.reeusda.gov/new/statepartners

Insects

Guidelines-Pests of Turfgrass
www.ipm.ucdavis.edu/PMG/selectnew
pest.turfgrass.html

Integrated Pest Management
wwwreeusda.gov.nipmn

RISE (Responsible Industry for a
Sound Environment)
www.pestfacts.org

Lawnmower Museums

Milton Keynes Museum
Milton Keynes (UK)
www.thg.org.uk/mkm.htm

A social, industrial, and agricultural history museum with a collection of nearly 70 mowers.

British Lawnmower Museum
Southport (UK)
dspace.dial.pipex.com/town/square/gf86/

Dedicated to the history of the lawn mower

Museum of Gardening History
London (UK)

This central London museum has a small selection of lawnmowers on display

The Reel Lawn Mower History & Preservation Project
Haydenville, MA

The collection was begun to preserve the hand, horse, and motor mowers of the 19th and early 20th centuries

Rural History Centre,
University of Reading (UK)

The UK's premier agricultural history resource, with a small selection of lawnmowers and extensive company archives

Media (Print and Electronic)

Athletic Turf Technology
Duluth, MN
www.landscapegroup.com
Phone: 800-346-0085

Golf Course Management
Grounds Maintenance Magazine
www.gcsaa.org/gcm/gcm_fr.html
www.grounds-mag.com
Phone: 913-341-1300

Home Lawn and Leisure
Phone: 802-748-8908

154

Landscape & Irrigation   Phone: 847-427-9512
Arlington Heights, IL

Landscape Management   www.landscapegroup.com
Duluth, MN   Phone: 800-346-0085

Lawn and Landscape   www.lawnandlandscape.com
Cleveland, OH   Phone: 800-456-0707

ProTurf Magazine   Phone: 937-644-0011
Marysville. OH

Sleeping Bear Press   www.sleepingbearpress.com
                                          Phone: 800-487-2323

SportsTURF   www.greenindustry.com/st/current

Turf   www.turfmagazine.com
St. Johnsbury, NJ   Phone: 802-748-8908

Turfgrass Trends   www.landscapegroup.com

Mowing
Safe Mowing Tips   opei.mow.org/Safety/index.html

Pesticides
Information Sheet   www.mda.state.md.us/plant/bmps.htm

Turfgrass Fungicide   www.ianr.unl.edu/ianr/pubs/

Trade Names   NEBFACTS/NF214.HTM

Seed
Applewood Wildflower Seed Co.   www.applewoodseed.com
P.O. Box 10761 Edgemont Station   Phone: 303-431-6283
Golden, CO 80401
They sell wildflower seed on a retail basis by mail; excellent seed; good customer service!

Arvada CO   Phone: 303-431-7333

Lofts Seed   www,turf.com

National Turfgrass Evaluation Program   www.ars-grin.gov/ars/Beltsville/
                                                 barc/psi/morris.htm

Turfgrass Species Selection   www.ohioline.ag.ohio-state.edu/hyg-fact/
                                                 4000/4011.html

National Wildflower Research Center   www.wildfloer.org
                                                 Phone: 512-292-4200

University Turf Programs
Clemson University   virtual.clemson.edu/groups/hort/
                                                 sctop/sctophom.htm

Colorado State Entomology Page   www.colostate.edu/Depts./
                                                 Entomology/ent.html

Cornell University   www.cals.cornell.edu/
                                                 dept/flori/turf/index.html

Guelph Turfgrass Institute   www.uoguelph.ca/GTI/gtihome.htm

Iowa State Entomology Page   www.public.iastate.edu/entomology

Kansas State University   www.oznet.ksu.edu/dp_hfrr/
                                                 turf/welcome.htm

Michigan State University   www.msu.edu/user/turf

Mississippi State University   www.msstate.edu/Dept/PSS/
                                                 public_html/golf.html

North Carolina State University   www.ces.ncsu.edu/TurfFiles/index.html

North Dakota State University   www.ag.ndsu.nodak.edu

Ohio State University	www.hcs.ohio-state.edu/hcs/turf.html
Oklahoma State University	www.okstate.edu/ag/asnr/hortla/hort_fac/martin/turf.htm
Oregon State University	www.forages.css.orst.edu
Penn State University	www.worldcampus.psu.edu/pub/programs/turfgrass
Purdue University	www.agry.purdue.edu/agronomy/turf/turf.htm
Rutgers University	aesop.rutgers.edu/www/cent-inst/turf.html
Texas A & M University	aggieturf.tamu.edu
Turfgrass Information Files (TGIF/MSU) *Excellent resource center of Michigan State University*	www.lib.msu.edu/tgif
University of Connecticut	www.canr.uconn.edu/CANR/plsci/agr-ts.htm
University of Arkansas	www.uark.edu/ArkHort
University of Florida	hort.ifas.ufl.edu/turf
University of Illinois	www.turf.uiuc.edu
University of Georgia	mars.cropsoil.uga.edu/fac_turf.htm
University of Kentucky	www.uky.edu/Agriculture/ukturf
University of Maine	www.ume.maine.edu/~nfa/lhc/hortic.htm
University of Maryland	iaa.umd.edu/umturf/umturf.html
University of Massachusetts	www.umass.edu/umext/programs/agro/turf_grass/
University of Missouri	www.missouri.edu/!extbsc/turf/turfhp.htm

University of Nebraska   hort.unl.edu/turf/index.html

University of Rhode Island   www.uri.edu/cels/pls/turf.html

University of Tennessee   web.utk.edu/~uthort/htm/commf.htm

University of Wisconsin   www.cals.wisc.edu/research/
research_stations11.html

Weather

CNN Weather   www.cnn.com/weather/index.html

Ohio State University   www.asp1.sbs.ohio-state.edu

National Weather Service   www.nws.noaa.gov

The Weather Channel   www.weather.com/twc/homepage.twc

Intellicast   www.intellicast.com

Weeds

Guidelines-Pests of Turfgrass   www.ipm.ucdavis.edu/PMG/selectnew
pest.turfgrass.html

Turfgrass Weeds   www.colostate.edu/Depts/IPM/natparks
/turfweed.html

World Weeds Database   ifs.plants.ox.ac.uk/wwd/pweeds.htm

Chapter 19
REFERENCES

Publications

Foth, Henry D. *Fundamentals of Soil Science*, Seventh Edition. New York: John Wiley & Sons, 1984.

Myers, Melinda. *The Garden Book for Wisconsin*. North Franklin, Tennessee: Cool Springs Press, 1999.

Puhalla, Jim, Jeff Krans, and Mike Goatley. *Sports Fields: A Manual for Design, Construction, and Maintenance*, Chelsea, Michigan: Ann Arbor Press, 1999

Turgeon, A.J. *Turfgrass Management, Revised Edition*. Virginia: Reson Publishing Co., Inc., 1985.

Vargas, J.M., Jr. *Management of Turfgrass Diseases*. Minneapolis, Minnesota: Burgess Publishing Company, 1981.

Walheim, Lance. *Lawn Care for Dummies*. New York: IDG Books Worldwide, Inc., 1998.

Wightman, S. "Masking Field Damage," STMA Conference presentation, January 2000.

Wignall, Jeff. "How to Take Winning Pictures," Photographic Products Group, New York: Eastman Kodak Company, 1985.

Web Pages

Barton, S. Garden Check, August 28, 1995, issue 10
http://bluehen.ags,udel.edu/deces/gc/1995/gc10-95.htm

Michigan State University Extension, Genesee County, Mowing Lawns, 4,1999 www.msu.edu/genesee/hort/mowinglawns.htm

Polomski, B. and Shaughnessy, D., Mowing Lawns, Clemson Extension Home and Garden Information Center, #1205
http://hgic.clemson.edu/Site1.htm

Polomski, B. and Shaughnessy, D., Lawn Establishment, Clemson Extension Home and Garden Information Center, #1203
http://hgic.clemson.edu/Site1.htm

Polomski, B. and Shaughnessy, D., Fertilizing Lawns, Clemson Extension Home and Garden Information Center, #1201
http://hgic.clemson.edu/Site1.htm

Reicher, Z. and Throssell, C. Control of Crabgrass in Homelawns, 3/1998 http://agry.purdue.edu/turf/pubs/ay10.htm

Relf, D. Guide to Nutrient Management, Consumer Horticulture, June 1996:Publication # 426-613
http://www.ext.vt.edu/pubs/enviohort/426-613.html

Smith, R. and Herman, D. Turfgrass Establishment and Maintenance for Home Lawns and Athletic Fields, May 1999; H-1170;
www.ext.nodak.edu/extpubs/plantsci/landscap/h1170.htm

Turfgrass Producers International, Turfgrass "Factoids," 1998-1999. Turf Resource Center www.turfgrasssod.org/trc/faqs.html

Turner, T.R. and Ricciute, P.J. Lawns and the Chesapeake Bay, Fact sheet 702 www.agnr.umd.edu/CES/Pubs/PDF/FS702.pdf

Voigt, T. Turfgrass Mowing, Turfgrass Extension Outreach,
www.turf.uiuc.edu/extension/ext-mow.html